This book is a must-read for anyone who works to make the critical connections between corporations and community. While service to less than privileged populations is her life work, Pam Erickson has dedicated herself to opening doors, maximizing opportunities, and making it easy for corporate America to share its bounty.

—B. J. HARRISON WAYMER
FOUNDER, B. J. WAYMER ASSOCIATES, INC.

As former president and chairman of Standard Textile Co., Inc., I have worked with Pam Erickson for many years by donating textile products to Operation Blessing, knowing that these products will be used wisely. Her compassion and dedication to helping the less fortunate are fantastic. It is my pleasure and good fortune to know Pam and Operation Blessing. Keep up your wonderful work.

—PAUL HEIMAN
STANDARD TEXTILE COMPANY

As an international lawyer and leader of a humanitarian nonprofit in Guatemala, I have been privileged to apply the principles contained in Pam's firsthand accounts of creating relationship mergers. These principles in this book have helped me fuse my work and my passion to serve humanity into one harmonious life journey.

—MARIO BUCARO
PARTNER, CENTRAL LAW

It has been my privilege to work closely with Pam in the nonprofit sector for many year~ She has been an innovator and an instrument for social cl

D1115157

to inspire the corporate and nonprofit communities to work together for the common good of those in need. This book captures much of her passion and creative methodology, inspiring the reader to become an agent for change in our society.

—Dave Phillips
President, Children's Hunger Fund

"Do you know where you are going to be leaving your mark?" This is one of the fundamental questions that author Pam Erickson asks and helps answer in her fine book, *You First, Me Second*. Erickson is able to share practical stories that exemplify the power of a shared vision, mutual respect, and open communication—these lead to "relationship mergers" that have a lifelong impact. *You First, Me Second* is a powerful work that leaders will find valuable.

—Carlos Campo
President, Regent University

Pam is right—"When the right people are motivated by the right reasons, they will do the right things." The problem often is that good people and organizations do not know what to do. That is the power of this book. It tells the stories of successful efforts by companies, nonprofits, and innovative people to make a difference in the world. Reading their stories should inspire all of us. Pam is just the person to tell us these stories. Her own work in serving the needs of people living in poverty around the world is an example in itself!

—Michael J. Nyenhuis
President and CEO, MAP International

Pam's efforts in relationship building helped us to engage our sponsors, players, fans, and hundreds of volunteers to serve our community. The Two Teams, One Goal event has become a highlight for the Kansas City Chiefs' and Royals' efforts to eradicate hunger in our city. In the process thousands of people received the assistance they needed. A true home run!

—BEN AKEN
SENIOR DIRECTOR, COMMUNITY RELATIONS,
KANSAS CITY ROYALS

you first,
me second

you first,
me second

PAM ERICKSON

Most CHARISMA HOUSE BOOK GROUP products are available at special quantity discounts for bulk purchase for sales promotions, premiums, fund-raising, and educational needs. For details, write Charisma House Book Group, 600 Rinehart Road, Lake Mary, Florida 32746, or telephone (407) 333-0600.

YOU FIRST, ME SECOND by Pam Erickson
Published by FrontLine
Charisma Media/Charisma House Book Group
600 Rinehart Road
Lake Mary, Florida 32746
www.charismahouse.com

Unless otherwise noted, all Scripture quotations are from the Holy Bible, New Living Translation, copyright © 1996, 2004, 2007. Used by permission of Tyndale House Publishers, Inc., Wheaton, IL 60189. All rights reserved.

Scripture quotations marked AMP are from the Amplified Bible. Old Testament copyright © 1965, 1987 by the Zondervan Corporation. The Amplified New Testament copyright © 1954, 1958, 1987 by the Lockman Foundation. Used by permission.

Visit the author's website at www.youfirstmesecond.com.

Cover design by Justin Evans
Design Director: Bill Johnson

Library of Congress Cataloging-in-Publication Data:
An application to register this book for cataloging has been submitted to the Library of Congress.

International Standard Book Number: 978-1-61638-968-0
E-book ISBN: 978-1-61638-969-7

First edition

13 14 15 16 17 — 9 8 7 6 5 4 3 2 1
Printed in the United States of America

This book is dedicated to my sister Lynda, who passed away in 2011 after a lengthy battle with cancer. Throughout my life she encouraged me to remain faithful, stay the course, and believe that dreams really do come true. Even though she's gone, her words still inspire me.

Contents

Acknowledgments

I WOULD LIKE TO express appreciation to my friend Michael Briggs, who is a living testimony of the selfless "you first, me second" lifestyle. His encouragement, sound counsel, and constant availability have been of incredible value to me.

Michael is a creative consultant who has worked with various companies and organizations for more than three decades, including the publishing and retail communities, parachurch organizations, and some of the largest ministries on the planet. As founder and president of Briggs Creative, Michael is a behind-the-scenes leader who helps to establish and refine strategies for an organization's growth and success. With his years of rubber-meets-the-highway experience, Michael brings a unique perspective to those he serves. He is truly one of a kind—the type of friend everyone needs on his team.

Foreword

N MY YOUNG life I have had the privilege of being surrounded by superstars. My father, Ronnie Lott, was an NFL
Hall of Famer and was on four Super Bowl teams filled with
superstars. In my own career I was surrounded by great athletes both in college and in my seven years as an NFL player.
But despite all the very talented players I have been around,
none compare to the individuals who make positive impacts in
the lives of others on a daily basis. These heroes and sheroes are
the true superstars who make our world a better place. In *You
First, Me Second* you will not only learn why Pam Erickson is
someone I respect, admire, and consider to be a superstar, but
you will also learn that no matter who you are or where you
are, you can be a superstar too. Pam and I have both learned
it's not what you have but what you give that affords you the
opportunity to be considered a superstar.

In this book Pam shares a number of stories about other
wonderful individuals who embrace the power of giving and
champion efforts to make a difference in their communities. As you read these pages, you will learn how others are
making the world better and in turn can apply what you have

learned in your daily life. Each chapter provides some practical insights to help encourage you to embrace these philosophies, which can become catalysts for performing acts of kindness. Every chapter describes a character trait—passionate, genuine, purpose driven, to name a few—that has helped propel others to become true superstars.

Pam has spent her life developing relationships and leveraging gifts and resources to make a difference in the lives of people around the world. As you read these stories, a flame will grow inside you and inspire you to make a difference in others' lives. We all lead very busy lives, and it's easy to become blind to the needs around us. But after reading this book, all your senses will be aware of the needs around you. I pray that you not only become aware of those needs, but that you also will begin to look for ways to meet them.

Do you want the world to become a better place? We all do, right? Well, like my friend Pam once told me, "Your world becomes better when people help people." I am so thankful Pam took the time to share with all of us these wonderful stories that will inspire us, motivate us, drive us, encourage us, and spur us on to become superstars!

—Ryan Nece
Former NFL player
Founder of the Ryan Nece Foundation

Introduction

WHEN I WAS twelve years old, my life was in turmoil. My mother, a single working mom struggling to provide for a family of five, was in a serious relationship that I knew would result in her eventual second marriage. I didn't like the idea of having a new father because I was waiting patiently for my "real" dad to come back home. I was at an awkward age marked by raging hormones and unpredictable emotional outbursts. I was only in the seventh grade, but already I was filled with anger, lashing out at everyone around me. My mom's concerns about my behavior were merited as she watched my grade in conduct plummet from an A to an F over the course of that school year. Yes, anyone who knew me could clearly see that I was a young girl in crisis.

However, there was one bright spot during those dark days. It was the day I wound up spending a warm, sunny May afternoon with someone I hardly knew. My mom had a friend from work named Ginny who took a special interest in me. I can only imagine what my mom had shared with Ginny about my unruly behavior, but as it turned out, it didn't scare her away. In fact, she asked me one day if I'd like to come over to her place and go swimming. I agreed to our outing even though I felt it was going to be a bit awkward for both of us.

At her apartment complex Ginny and I lounged outside, enjoying the sun and taking an occasional refreshing dip in the pool. We didn't do much talking at first, but it wasn't long before we were fully engaged in conversation. It all started as I was reading through a short story from one of her magazines. Ginny asked me if I liked to read.

"Oh, yes," I replied, "and I love to write too!" My answer began a discussion between us about some of my favorite books, and I even told her all about a mystery story I had written the year before. For at least an hour I did most of the talking while Ginny listened intently. At various points she appropriately interjected relevant questions that encouraged me to keep sharing.

Before I knew it, the afternoon sun had begun to set, and Ginny said she needed to get me home. I recall feeling disappointed and wishing we didn't have to go. As it turned out, that one afternoon was the only time I ever spent with Ginny. We made no plans to see each other again or even to catch up occasionally by phone. No, that one brief encounter was all we had together, but to this day, many decades later, I hold our conversation very dear to my heart.

What made this meeting so significant to me? Why have I never forgotten it? It was because Ginny made my needs her only focus. For one afternoon the only thing that mattered to Ginny was me.

When Ginny first heard my mom talk about me and my rebellious ways, she seized the opportunity to help me by rearranging her schedule and making me her priority. She invested her time to help me talk through the issues that were causing me to be so troubled. She listened intently and made me feel comfortable enough not only to open up but also to even share with her my hopes and dreams. Because of her tender, nonjudgmental acceptance of me I felt she genuinely cared.

Ginny's questions were filled with interest, and as we spoke, her concern for me helped me begin to believe that I really mattered. Ginny knew I was in tremendous need of affirmation and encouragement. That day, as we sat beside her pool, she carefully shared words I needed to hear—words that would uplift and, yes, even inspire me to turn my attitude around. Ginny gave me confidence that I could start fresh with a better outlook for my future.

I'm sure Ginny never thought our brief time together would remain a part of me for decades to come. But because she was willing to respond to my need, I became a very different young girl. If asked how I would describe Ginny, without hesitation I would say that she was a "you first, me second" person.

People Helping People

Ginny chose that summer day to give me the gift of her time and attention though she had no idea her one act of kindness would have such a profound impact on me. Her demonstration of value toward me led me to dedicate my life to doing the same for others, initially as a teacher and now as part of the staff of Operation Blessing International. In my position at the global humanitarian relief organization I've secured donations of food, relief supplies, and medicine to help meet the needs of those suffering around the world.

Throughout my years of service I have met many other people like Ginny. These individuals consistently put others' needs before their own, performing acts of kindness without expecting anything in return. I like to call these individuals, selfless, "you first, me second" people because they freely offer their help and give of themselves whether anyone is watching or not. They choose to intervene in the lives of those in need of assistance even if only for brief moments. They are everyday people who make an extraordinary impact on those around them, people just like:

- The hospice volunteer who quietly sits and strokes the hair of one who is dying

- The woman who spends the entire day on her knees scrubbing the baseboards of the house her friend has to put up for sale

- The teacher who gives up her summers to teach so that children who have fallen through the cracks can have a second chance to learn

- The community leader who offers free counseling services for traumatized and abandoned children

- The pastor who opens up his church after hours so that those who have no place to sleep can find safe refuge

- The mom who consistently drives for more than her share of carpooling trips and never utters a word of complaint

- The three-hundred-pound NFL player who spends his day off bagging groceries that will be given to those in his community who are hungry and in need

- The sweet potato farmer who makes sure he gives the firstfruits of his crop to charity

- The policeman who keeps blankets in his car in case he comes across someone during the night who is cold and alone

- The grandmother who takes care of her grandchildren free of charge to ease her daughter's financial worries

- The son who is dedicated to honoring his widowed, aging mother through the assurance of his love and ongoing presence in her life

- The Little League coach who shows up for practices even when the kids on his team don't

- The widow on a fixed income who gives faithfully every month toward the needs of others

- The coworker who unexpectedly drops off bags of clothes on the porch of her friend so she will have a few more outfits to wear to work

- The boss who anonymously slips an envelope filled with much-needed cash under an employee's desk blotter

- The woman who prepares a covered dish to take to someone who is bedridden

- The man who is always willing to fix broken household items, repair cars that have quit running, or provide free on-call mechanical assistance when needed

- The little girl who uses her entire summer's allowance to buy school supplies for another little girl she's never met

The list could go on and on. These "you first, me second" people have chosen to live each day with the Golden Rule as their standard: they do unto others what they would want done to them.

If people were to describe you, what do you think they would they say? Perhaps they would start by listing your physical characteristics, such as your gender, your hair and eye color, your height and weight—all typical identifiers on driver's licenses and passports. If asked to describe your personality, people might use adjectives such as nice, friendly, funny, smart, serious, quiet, energetic, or boisterous.

But what if people were asked to describe the kind of person you are? Perhaps they would describe you as honest, sincere, reliable, genuine, or trustworthy. Or maybe they would say "dedicated" or "kind" to best frame your character. The traits you demonstrate by your words and actions will ultimately define who you are.

The "you first, me second" lifestyle is not reserved for a select few. It is for anyone willing to make more meaningful connections to bring positive change in someone's life. These meaningful connections are what I like to call relationship mergers—people helping people—and they occur in a variety of ways. They can originate in the workplace when teams gather to develop ways for employees to volunteer to benefit the community. They can occur when the leaders of local organizations donate resources to assist those in dire need of help.

Relationship mergers can be initiated when a mom or dad encourages a child to explore ways to demonstrate kindness to a neighbor. They can begin within a church when it encourages members to join in its community outreach efforts. Relationship mergers can even occur spontaneously when one person is prompted to stop by the side of the road to help a stranger change a flat tire.

Today *social responsibility* has become a buzzword as people become more aware not only of global issues but also of the everyday needs of those around us. The core meaning of social responsibility is that each of us is obligated to act in ways that will benefit society. But the *heart* of social responsibility is to make the time to meet people's needs not because we have to but because we want to.

Every day we reveal traits within our character through the choices we make, the words we speak, and the actions we take toward others. It's how we have been designed to reflect God's love for all mankind. Our outward expressions of love for our neighbors demonstrate our value for those we are serving, and they ultimately define our character. As each of us embraces the *heart* of social responsibility, we will become the people God created us to be.

Every day we make choices about the words we speak and the actions we take. If our friends ask us to meet them early on a Saturday morning, *dependability* will cause us to forgo sleeping in to arrive on time. If we are planning to have lunch with a friend and he is on a strict diet, *kindness* would move us to order food that we know he would be able to eat. When choosing to buy a birthday gift for a loved one, *thoughtfulness* will guide us to select the present that best reveals how much we value that person.

Our character guides the decisions we make. This book will help you to develop the character traits and positive attributes that will best equip you to effectively serve others. *You First, Me Second* features sixteen chapters, each one focused on a unique attribute found in a "you first, me second" person. Each trait is first explained and then illustrated through stories of real people who have put the needs of others first. Within these stories you will find examples of relationship mergers between everyday individuals who were in the right place at the right time to demonstrate the right response.

Examples will include community-minded businessmen and women, employee volunteers with a mission to make a difference, nonprofit workers dedicated to serving others, community leaders advocating for their neighbors, and many more, all dedicated to embracing a "you first, me second" lifestyle in their quest to touch hearts and effect change. I've had the privilege of knowing or personally observing all the people highlighted in these pages, and I can attest to their acts of compassion and their commitment to community. Their stories are sure to motivate and encourage you to boldly step out and create your own "love your neighbor" legacy.

The final section of each chapter provides creative ideas and practical suggestions for developing "you first, me second" character in your own life. This book will be your blueprint, helping you to define your core purpose and to start reaching out to serve those in need.

Many people want to make a difference, but often they don't know how. *You First, Me Second* is a *resource* to help you serve more effectively. If you have not yet begun to serve, this book will be your *guide* to getting started. Or if you once served but no longer do, *You First, Me Second* will be your *inspiration* to begin serving again.

The needs around us are enormous—they may even seem overwhelming at times. But in these pages you will find tools that will empower you to make a real difference. It is possible to bring about positive change in this world. It all begins when you choose to live "you first, me second."

Chapter 1

Being Purpose Driven

For the whole law can be summed up in this one
command: "Love your neighbor as yourself."
Galatians 5:14

THERE IS NOTHING more satisfying in life than having a sense of purpose. One of my favorite Bible verses is Philippians 3:10, and I love the way it reads in the Amplified version: "[For my determined purpose is] that I may know Him [that I may progressively become more deeply and intimately acquainted with Him, perceiving and recognizing and understanding the wonders of His Person...]." The verse boldly states that our determined purpose is to know God.

Jesus clearly says in the first and greatest commandment that knowing God is our most important priority (Matt. 22:37–38). He tells us to love God with all our heart, soul, and mind. Essentially every part of our being should be engaged in loving God, and the more we invest ourselves in that pursuit, the more we will come to know Him.

Philippians 3:10 also tells us that knowing God is a process: "That I may progressively become more deeply and intimately acquainted with Him" (AMP). Getting to know God is a journey, a progressive movement that leads us to grow deeper in our relationship with Him. As you focus your individual faith walk on your purpose—to know God—you will grow from within, and that growth will produce strong character traits such as integrity, honesty, kindness, gentleness, and patience, just to name a few.

As you grow in character as an individual, the second greatest commandment to "love your neighbor as yourself" (Matt. 22:39) makes more sense. It is the outflow of what you personally receive through knowing and loving God that is then revealed through acts of kindness toward your neighbors.

Loving yourself is not a matter of pride. It is actually a confidence in who you are and who God created you to be. Loving yourself equips you to give away the love you've received from God through deeds of service to others. In this way your life becomes purpose driven. When you fulfill the command to love your neighbor by using whatever gifts and talents you've been given to benefit others, you will be pleasing God by taking a "you first, me second" approach to making this world a better place.

When you are purpose driven to love and serve those in your community, the needs you focus on and your availability to serve may fluctuate, depending on your circumstances. What is vital, though, is that you are willing to be used to help meet needs, even at a moment's notice.

For example, if you are about to go shopping with a friend, and just as you are ready to walk out the door you get a call from someone who needs transportation to an appointment, would you change your plans? Or what if you are standing in line to check out at the grocery store, and the woman in front of you doesn't have enough money to cover the groceries she's trying to purchase? If you have the money, would you offer to cover her purchases, or would you watch as she goes through the embarrassment of removing items from her bag and having them subtracted from her bill?

When you stay flexible enough to meet needs because serving others is a priority, you can live out your purpose to love God over and over and over every day. You will be available for a coworker who needs to unload the burden of her financial struggles or to run an errand for the widow across the street or to make (or buy) cookies for the college kids at church. Performing small kindnesses such as these can help sharpen our focus on others and guide us toward becoming purpose driven. By recognizing that "needs" come in all shapes and sizes, we will become even more alert to opportunities to serve and thus more readily available to help out when needed.

Sometimes opportunities to live out our purpose come from out of nowhere, such as when we experience a serious life interruption. If you discover that one of your family members has breast cancer, suddenly your attention is diverted to learning more about the dreaded disease. You spend hours searching the Internet to gather the latest medical information and facts about the specific kind of breast cancer afflicting your loved one. More than likely you will reach out to your friends, neighbors, or coworkers to find out what they might know about the disease. You realize that your purpose now is to make your family's needs your priority.

As your family member walks through the grueling process of battling the disease, you may find yourself becoming a powerful supporter in the fight against breast cancer. You might decide to participate in a community 5K to help raise funds for breast cancer research or to devote your time engaging in other activities to help build awareness of the disease. The most important thing to remember is simply to remain available to meet the needs that will arise out of life's struggles. Your acts of service will allow you to demonstrate love to your neighbor in the fullest measure possible.

There may be times when we become so purpose driven regarding a specific cause that we become unstoppable in our determination to make a difference. Our ambition rises up from within us to become a force that is destined to bring positive change in people's lives. Sometimes we even surprise ourselves when our positive, can-do attitudes cause us to become determined to do whatever it takes to make something happen. No matter what our age, when we embrace a purpose-driven mind-set, our goal becomes to accomplish the impossible.

Even as an eleven-year-old girl I had the same passion and zeal that has made me the determined, purpose-driven person I am today. Here is my story.

My Purpose Birthed

I grew up in a home in which my mom, a single mother of four, worked a full-time job. We lived in Washington DC in the end unit of a long block of row houses, where a narrow alley served as my makeshift playground. We struggled financially, but as a young girl I never remember feeling poor.

My oldest sister, Lynda, and my big brother, John, played a huge part in creating a security bubble around me. As teenagers both of them juggled their school schedules so they could work part-time, and on every payday, without fail, they both willingly signed over their entire checks to my mom. Through those lean years my mom kept her ironclad will and dogged determination to hold our family of five together, no matter what. She worked long hours, and I, as the youngest in the family, along with a sister who was a year older than me, became typical latchkey kids. When my sister and I got home from school, we had assigned chores to do, and if we wanted to leave the house, we needed to call my mom and ask for her permission. Most of the time I did my homework and then took a break to watch a little television before starting my chores.

My mom's schedule didn't change during the summers, and neither did ours. We still had daily chores to do and rules to follow, but I did find myself watching more than my fair share of television. The summer after I finished the fifth grade, I happened to catch a special program on TV about muscular dystrophy and its devastating effects, especially on children. It was the first time I had ever heard of the disease, and I remember that as I watched the program, I felt a little frightened.

During the program I learned that a person could host a backyard carnival to help raise money for those afflicted with the disease. When I saw children my own age confined to wheelchairs and suffering from an ailment I could barely pronounce, I felt a surge of compassion within me that could not be contained. My heart became captivated with the carnival idea, and my purpose began to unfold. With tears welling up in my eyes and a sense of urgency in my heart, I ran outside to find my friends and to tell them all about what I had seen. I could barely catch my breath as I shared the carnival details, and in just a few minutes the group was ready to transform our back alley into a passageway of purpose.

I contacted the muscular dystrophy organization and requested information about hosting a backyard carnival. In less than a week we received an information packet with plenty of flyers and posters to post around the neighborhood. I remember being so excited when our package arrived that as I darted across the street, I ran into a tree. That caused me some downtime, a butterfly stitch, and a little embarrassment in front of my friends. However, in no time our little team of "spitfire marketers" was so convinced that we were going to have the best carnival in town that we even contacted the local newspapers and television stations to tell them about our event.

To get our booths ready, we found old appliance boxes and cut them up to create a beanbag toss and a "fishing" booth. When we were almost finished decorating the front of the game booths, all of a sudden I realized we didn't have any prizes for our winners. None of us had any money to buy prizes, and I had already convinced my friends' moms to bake cupcakes and cookies to sell on the day of the carnival. The two thoughts that kept running through my head were, "How are we going to raise money for muscular dystrophy if nobody will play our games?" and "Who will want to play games without any prizes?"

I didn't let those worries consume me, though. Instead, I took a deep breath and with my head held high, I voiced a determined resolution to walk to the nearest mall and ask for prize donations. At that very moment I was transformed from a pint-sized girl to a purpose-driven ambassador with a relentless will to accomplish my mission: the successful acquisition of prizes for our games.

That day I launched my first journey to "plead the cause" on behalf of those with muscular dystrophy. My sister Jackie accompanied me on the half-mile walk to the nearest shopping center. The two of us skipped along the way, carrying an empty box between us in anticipation of our success.

As we visited each store, I told the managers about the carnival, the afflicted children, our plan to raise money by playing different games, and then our critical shortage of prizes to give to the winners. I spoke with the boldness of a warrior, and one by one, each manager gave a generous selection of merchandise that we could use for our prizes. In no time at all our box was filled to the brim with prizes, and for the first time I experienced the power of relationship mergers.

I knew that each of the managers had caught my vision, and through their donations I had become the conduit connecting their resources to the need. The excitement of sharing with each of the store managers about the need to raise money for muscular dystrophy placed a desire in me to continue creating relationship mergers to benefit people struggling through hardship in their lives. That experience launched me toward who I am today: an advocate for the poor who have no voice.

Our carnival turned out to be a great success. We raised more cash than any of us ever imagined we would. Our contribution to the muscular dystrophy organization was the second highest total turned in that summer. The event that began with a vision grew into a reality. In our little team the focus was never on ourselves; each of us had personally embraced the needs of the children we were driven to help.

As a purpose-driven eleven-year-old girl I somehow knew that this was going to be my destiny.

Today I am the vice president of procurement and corporate relations at Operation Blessing, a position that allows me to be a full-time advocate for the needs of people around the world. Every day I approach companies, businesses, and nonprofit organizations asking for donations of resources to be used for the benefit of people and community programs. I am living out the destiny God placed in my heart so many years ago—and I'm loving it!

I've embraced Proverbs 31:9 as my life scripture: "Yes, speak up for the poor and helpless, and see that they get justice." I must say that through the many years of speaking up for those who are poor and in need, it has not always been as easy as was my venture to acquire prize donations for my carnival. Indeed there have been occasions on which it has taken me more than a year to finally receive a company's donated resources. With speaking up for the poor and helpless as my purpose, I am compelled to keep looking for food, medicine, relief supplies, and other provisions for those who are caught in the cycle of suffering.

When you run into the challenge of getting those negative responses, and you're waiting and hoping to receive product donations, anchor deep and find your wellspring of strength. Recognize that the rejection is not personal and regroup. You will discover that it is indeed possible to consistently present yourself in a respectful position of asking again and again and again.

When you are driven by your purpose, you will be strengthened in your love, joy, peace, patience, kindness, faith, humility, or self-control. Whatever quality you need at a given moment for your relationship with a donor to remain open will be built into your communication with that person. And that quality will define the essence of your character as you continue to plead the cause of those in need.

The following story is about a relationship that I cultivated on my instrument of choice: the phone. I conversed with a person for well over a year before donations from his organization came our way, but the relationship that was built during that waiting period is precious to me and something I will forever treasure.

Joe's Story

My very first conversation with Joe took place when I made a cold call in hopes of receiving donations from a warehouse facility that Joe managed. Joe answered the phone, and our conversation was over not long after it started. I had asked him if we might be considered for a donation, and he had replied with an emphatic no. But I had kindly asked if I could call him again at another time, and to my surprise he said, "OK."

Following that initial call, I wondered if it might be a good idea to remove him from my cold call list and just move on to the next person. However, something in me did not want to give up. Perhaps I was motivated by the challenge.

About two weeks later I called Joe back. I was surprised that he remembered me. I still got the no response to my request for donations, but surprisingly Joe said he would put me on the waiting list for groups seeking to be put on the official list of recipient organizations. I jumped at the chance to be on that waiting list. When I asked Joe what number I was on the list, he said, "Thirteen out of thirteen." I thought that was a good start, and I genuinely thanked him for the privilege of at least being put on a list for consideration! Surprisingly he told me to check back in two weeks to see where we were on the list.

Like clockwork I checked in with Joe about every two weeks. In subsequent conversations we both became comfortable enough in our relationship to even share a few corny jokes. I must admit, though, that every time I made my call, my heart was pounding with anticipation that this would be the time he'd offer us a donation. Several months after my initial call we were finally put on the official recipient list, but then we had to wait for our turn to receive a donation. During those additional months of waiting and checking in, my conversations with Joe went from a call for a donation to a dialogue between two people who appreciated each other's sense of humor and outlook on life.

One day, instead of having to proactively contact him, I actually received a surprise call from Joe to let me know that he finally had a donation for me! We both laughed at how long it had taken—over a year—but I would not trade the phone calls with Joe that led up to the donation for anything in this world.

When we picked up that first donation, I made sure that I personally tracked Joe's product from the time it was released to us until the final transfer into the hands of the people who needed it most. I sent Joe some stories from individuals who had received his donations of food and other household items. Many of them shared the compelling details of their personal struggles and how much the donation had meant to them. I knew Joe's heart was touched by their stories.

One time Joe called me and asked if I knew of anyone who needed shoes. He had been cleaning out a top section of the warehouse and found a pallet full of new children's shoes. He said the boxes looked pretty bad but that the shoes were in perfect condition. As it turned out, only moments before he called, I had received an e-mail from the director of a Romanian orphanage who had asked me if there was any chance that we had children's shoes available.

When I told Joe "the rest of the story" about the need for shoes in Romania, he couldn't believe it. He was so taken aback by the timing of his call and my e-mail from Romania that he literally was speechless! From that time on Joe became linked at the heart to meeting the needs of people around the world.

After two years of a great relationship between Joe and me, he retired from his warehouse job. Shortly before his last day at work I asked him if I could drive up to see him and take him out to lunch. He said he could not leave the warehouse, so I asked if I could bring lunch to him. We both agreed that it would be great to see each other before he left, so I found out his favorite foods and packed them up in a special picnic lunch.

When I arrived, there was no place to sit inside the warehouse, so we went outdoors, where I made a makeshift table setting by spreading a cloth across a concrete slab. As we shared lunch, we reminisced about the many times Joe's donations had arrived just in time to be instrumental in meeting very specific needs.

As a farewell present I gave Joe a Bible with his name engraved on the front. I told him that with the number of times he had been the vital link to caring for the poor, his involvement had to be God's perfect timing, so maybe someday he would like to read more about the God who had been watching over him. When I left Joe that day, reflecting on our time together, I couldn't help but feel like I had just dined with a king in the midst of concrete and packaged food.

My relationship with Joe began with a couple of words shared in a very short phone conversation. Who would have thought it would result in a rock-solid relationship by which so many people would benefit? Joe made me a promise the day as we dined together on that chunk of concrete. He told me that before he left his job, he would make sure the decision-makers at his company knew about the integrity of our organization and the genuine people on our staff. His commitment to take care of us has since resulted in millions of pounds of incredible product being loyally donated to our community partners across America.

Even though Joe and I no longer stay in touch, I know that wherever he is, he's making this world a better place. And I'm sure the hundreds of thousands of people who have been impacted by the donations we've received through the years would unanimously agree. When I reflect on my thoughts after that first conversation with Joe, I am most thankful that I didn't proceed with my first inclination to cross his name off my list. I am eternally grateful that I found the strength within to stay focused on leading the charge as a purpose-driven advocate for the poor.

Living "You First, Me Second"

"You first, me second" people live by a set of principles that make them distinguishable from the rest of the world. Let your purpose be driven by the power from within your being. When your own life reflects integrity and strength of character, you will become more available to serve others with purpose and conviction. Do any of the following principles of character describe you? Answer yes or no.

- Do you say what you mean?
- Can you be counted on?
- Do you pay your bills on time?
- Are you fair?
- Do you compromise when you shouldn't?
- Do you keep your word?
- Do you gossip?
- Do you put in an honest day's work?
- Are you teachable?
- Are you respectful?
- Do you finish what you start?

If any of the characteristics above are not currently part of your lifestyle, identify the areas in which you need to see improvement. If it is possible, ask a friend or loved one to help you work through the list to see if their assessment agrees with yours.

I opened this chapter with a statement: "Our determined purpose is to know God." In order for this to occur, there must be movement on your part toward a deeper and more intimate relationship with God. He wants it, and you need it. Find the time to study biblical principles that will strengthen you on the inside so that you will extend the benefits of that strength outwardly to those who need it most. Think of it as spiritual CPR. Inhale God's words, and then exhale through your deeds.

A great way to get you into the study of God's Word is to do a topical study on each one of the principles listed above. I have relisted the principles and have identified the topic associated with each one below. Make sure that you have a study Bible that lists various topics along with corresponding scriptures.

- You say what you mean (integrity).
- You can be counted on (reliability).
- You pay your bills on time (uprightness).
- You are fair (justice).
- You won't compromise (steadfastness).
- You keep your word (trustworthiness).
- You will not gossip (gossiping).
- You put in an honest day's work (honesty).
- You are teachable (humility).
- You are respectful (reverence).
- You finish what you start (discipline).

As you progressively move forward in your journey to know God, your inward character will develop into the strength you need to love your neighbor the way God intends. As God Himself shapes your character, He will also become the one driving your purpose.

Chapter 2

Being an Encourager

Let us think of ways to motivate one another
to acts of love and good works.
Hebrews 10:24

To ENCOURAGE SOMEONE is to inspire him with confidence. Everybody loves to be around encouragers. Encouragers are the kind of people who ooze positivism. The love of life that encouragers can generate naturally creates an atmosphere of anticipation and celebration. Those who spend time with encouragers are sure to benefit from their overflow of optimism, as they bring enough energy to the scene to stimulate even the most melancholy setting.

Encouragers have a magnetic charisma that can pull anyone out of a funk. They can effectively instill confidence and a sense of ironclad strength in others to help them believe that nothing is impossible. Their example of living life to the fullest often leads others to pursue the same.

Encouragers know just what to say and exactly when to say it to inspire confidence in someone who has a defeated spirit. Encouragers have a hearty supply of laughter and quickly transform the gloominess of a dismal day into hopeful enthusiasm. They know how to refresh the hearts and minds of those around them.

Through the investment of their time and energy, encouragers pump life back into the wearied soul. We should all have at least one encourager in our midst who knows how to lift our spirits when we're down. There's nothing like having someone in your life you can count on to say or do something to cheer you on when times get tough.

Encouragers paint a picture of what could be and then spur others on to believe in themselves enough to take the first step toward their dreams. Has someone in your life encouraged you? Take a moment to reflect on what it meant to be on the receiving end of that encouragement and the impact it has had on your life.

Have you been helped through a difficult time by someone who believed in you? Has someone ever urged you to try something new that turned out to be exactly what you needed to change the course of your life? Were you by chance prompted to accomplish something you once thought impossible? I had a friend named Betty whose encouragement did just that for me!

"You First, Me Second" Encouragement

It started one summer when my family moved to a college town in central Texas. Betty and I met at church, and I found out that she was a professor at the local university. I told her that I had always wanted to go to college, but since I was a military wife with two small children, I had decided that it was too late. Betty immediately responded by telling me that I could do anything once I put my mind to it. I had heard that statement before, but at this point I was convinced that college was too lofty a goal.

But Betty wouldn't let me settle for believing college was impossible for me. Instead she filled me up with "what ifs," and before long I began to believe that I really could go to college. During the following weeks Betty invested her time in guiding me through the college admissions process, giving me a tour of the university campus and speaking as if I were already enrolled. She and I spent time brainstorming to find a course of study that would be perfectly suited for me, and before I knew it, I was registered for the fall semester as an incoming freshman—when I was nearly twice the age of my fellow class-mates. How had that happened?

As an encourager Betty helped me to believe in myself. During some of those first college courses, it was tough for me to stay focused and not to feel overwhelmed. One time I remember facing a monumental mental hurdle. About three weeks into a basic college math course I became thoroughly convinced that I was going to fail. Betty would not let me give up. Even though she could do the math problems in her sleep, she committed to tutor me every day as I plowed through what seemed like endless pages of numbers.

Betty and I sat down each afternoon and worked through every problem until I could not only solve each one on my own but also understand the steps it took to get the answers. I wound up passing the math course with flying colors, and I know it was because of Betty's encouragement. Betty taught me to not give up and to remain focused on my goal. Her encouragement and confidence in my abilities inspired me to look at life with a new set of eyes. Betty left her mark on my life, as encouragers often do for others, by investing herself in me and giving me the gift of her time.

Not long after I started college, Betty was diagnosed with cervical cancer. She fought a gallant battle, but after only eighteen short months she passed away. During her fight she exemplified bravery and courage. Betty's legacy beats on in the hearts of those she encouraged to continue running the race of life with spirit and confidence. I am only one of many who was positively impacted by Betty's "you first, me second" approach to life. She constantly made herself available to encourage the hearts of those who needed it most.

Encouragers can be influential leaders. They know how to inspire their teams to achieve greatness by instilling the confidence within each person that his contribution to the group is not only needed but also wanted. The positive outlook of an encouraging leader can woo people to join that person in creating a team that is committed to giving a project its best effort. These encouragers have the ability to achieve goals by inspiring everybody in their group to participate and by giving each team member a voice. They can effectively instill confidence in others by firmly believing that as their team works together, nothing is impossible.

I have had the pleasure of working with an encouraging team leader who will go down in history as a legendary example of how to live life to the fullest. His legacy of influence will surely impact generations to come. I met Reggie White when he was the defensive tackle for the Green Bay Packers. Our meeting centered on the issue of hunger relief and how to serve at-risk communities—neighborhoods with low incomes, low high school graduation rates, and high unemployment—across America. Here is his story.

Reggie White,
the "Minister of Defense"

An article on the Internet caught my eye. It was about the community investment efforts the Campbell's Soup Company was leading through a partnership with Reggie White. Reggie had been selected as Campbell's Chunky soup's spokesperson of the year. The article stated that the football player would be earning donated cans of soup from Campbell's—twenty thousand cans for every tackle and fifty thousand for every sack he made during the regular season. All the cans of Chunky soup that Reggie earned would be donated to a national food bank network.[*]

Being an avid football fan, I knew that Reggie would surely be earning a lot of cans over the course of the entire season. Operation Blessing also worked with hunger relief, but since it was not a part of the food bank network receiving the donations, I wanted to ask Reggie if some of the soup he earned could be donated to us as well.

So I wrote Reggie a letter on behalf of the hungry people across America whom our organization served. The letter explained that we too had a national hunger relief program that served thousands of people, and I asked Reggie if organizations like those within our network would be able to receive some of the donated soup.

---

[*] *Philadelphia Business Journal*, "Reggie White Tackles Soup Labels," September 2, 1997, http://www.bizjournals.com/philadelphia/stories/1997/09/01/daily2.html (accessed December 12, 2012).

After finishing the letter, I sought out the best way to get it to Reggie before the plans for the soup can donations were solidified. After making multiple phone calls and networking with the Green Bay Packers' community relations department, I was given Reggie's fax number. I took a deep breath, crossed my fingers, said a prayer, and then faxed the letter.

Within a day I heard from Reggie's personal assistant, who told me that Reggie had read the letter and that he wanted to give our organization some of his earned cans. What an encouragement it was for me to hear those words! The assistant gave me the name and phone number of Reggie's agent. The rest is an incredible story of how the request for donated cans evolved into a huge multistate project that encouraged thousands of people living in underserved communities across the country.

During one of my conversations with Reggie's agent, I learned that Reggie had suggested that I visit Campbell's headquarters and discuss the details of the donation with the marketing team in charge of the program. I made some calls, flew to Newark, New Jersey, and then drove to the city of Camden, the home of Campbell's corporate offices. There I met Syd, who was part of the team that had created Reggie's Chunky soup television commercial.

The commercial was definitely a product of advertising brilliance—if you saw it, you remembered it. Reggie's mother was featured as a Green Bay Packer cheerleader. She popped out of the overhead luggage compartment on an airplane holding a can of Campbell's Chunky soup in her hand and urging everyone to join Reggie and the team in seeing to it that Campbell's Chunky soup cans were in kitchen cupboards across America. Syd and his team had done a fabulous job. I wound up having a great meeting, during which all the people I met encouraged me to continue to focus on meeting hunger needs across America.

As a result of a fabulous football season in which he made numerous tackles and sacks, Reggie earned more than a million cans of Chunky soup. He fulfilled his promise to us by giving us multiple truckloads of soup cans as part of the generous donation from Campbell's soup, a company truly committed to community investment. When we distributed the cans to hunger relief organizations and food pantries, the encouragement coming from people was incredible. The hearts touched through the generosity of both Campbell's and Reggie were too numerous to count. But the story doesn't end there.

The following year was Reggie's final season as a Green Bay Packer. Because our organization led a strong domestic hunger relief program and because it was Reggie's last year playing at Lambeau Field, Reggie and I discussed hosting a food distribution event in each of the cities where the Packers were playing away games that season. Because of his "you first, me second" mind-set Reggie wanted this to be a special commemoration of his love for people and to serve as encouragement to those experiencing economic difficulties across the country.

The details that would need to be managed seemed overwhelming. However, it wasn't long before Reggie, with his big smile and encouraging words, had me thoroughly convinced that the job could be done. As a result, I took a step of faith, and together Reggie and I organized large community food-distribution events in eight different cities during Reggie's final season as a Green Bay Packer.

Because of Reggie's heart for people, the impact of the combined events that season was overwhelming. More than sixteen thousand people received the encouraging message that someone cared about them. Even when there was inclement weather, large crowds of people waited patiently in line to receive the food they knew would make a difference to their families. Directors of church food pantries, community feeding-program leaders, and volunteers from local food banks were buzzing with excitement. Indeed, Reggie encouraged people to believe that even in hard times, there is a reason for hope.

The season's final event took place in a parking lot in Green Bay on a snowy Wisconsin day on which the temperature plummeted to nine degrees Fahrenheit. Even the freezing temperatures did not keep people in need of food from coming to the site. I remember one family with at least four small children who huddled close together to stay warm while waiting in line. A little girl in the middle of the cluster not only had no coat but also was scantily clothed in light pants and a sleeveless blouse. I gasped in horror, and just as I was about to move toward the family, I caught sight of a volunteer who had been helping distribute groceries taking off her coat and immediately giving it to the little girl.

It was a spontaneous act of kindness that literally took my breath away, and watching it occur right in front of my eyes will most assuredly keep this great example of human compassion indelibly stamped in my memory. It was not long after I witnessed this special moment that I saw the same woman sobbing on the shoulder of one of her friends. With a voice of brokenness she sighed that she could not believe that the need was so great right in her own backyard. She wasn't going to stop with just the Green Bay Packer event. She was determined to do more, and that day would only be the beginning of her journey to make a difference in her community. Reggie's encouragement to reach out to communities in need inspired this woman to continue the work that he had started.

After his banner year with the Packers, Reggie moved on, but his encouragement had spurred other teams to carry on his legacy of NFL community food distributions. The program, now well over a decade later, still has the signature of Reggie's smile and his generous heart.

It was a day of great sadness for all of us when we learned of Reggie's sudden passing. Not long after Reggie's death, I received a call from Campbell's Soup letting me know that they wanted to donate cans of soup to Operation Blessing in Reggie's honor. They asked if we would be able to help them make that happen, and I gave them my assurance that we would be honored to help in any way we could. I made an inquiry call and found out that we could deliver the donated soup cans to a pantry in Green Bay that was the same location where we had once hosted a community food distribution. I reassured Campbell's Soup that we would be able to deliver their donation as soon it was ready to be picked up.

Not long afterward one of our fifty-three-foot tractor-trailers was at the dock of Campbell's distribution center to pick up the donated cans. The encouragement now extended from the heart and soul of our organization to include those on the Campbell's Soup staff as well as the incredible people serving the community in Green Bay. We all came together to unite for one purpose—to remember the impact of Reggie's life on so many.

Reggie was an encourager who not only inspired his fellow players but also lifted the hearts of community workers across

America by tangibly supporting their work. His encouragement ignited the spirits of those committed to care for the needs of people in their own cities. You see, there are times when community work can become overwhelming, entailing long hours with little sleep. There can be days in which caring for those living in poverty or struggling through crushing circumstances can become so burdensome that you may wonder if you have the stamina to continue. This is where Reggie brought hope to the hearts of pastors, lay leaders, and volunteers serving communities across the country. He was like a physician who prescribed the perfect dose of encouragement to bring recovery, refreshment, and restoration to thousands of weary souls.

In life Reggie White was an encourager, and in his death he continues to leave a legacy of influence. That's what encouragers do. They make a difference, change their world—and spur people on to do great things.

Living "You First, Me Second"

There are three qualities that all encouragers share. First, they notice the people around them. Second, they are initiators, often spontaneously speaking words that will uplift others or doing deeds for the benefit of someone else. Third, if a person's need turns out to be long-term, encouragers invest their time to reaffirm their commitment to others. To help develop the encourager in you, let's take a closer look at each of these qualities.

Notice the people around you.

- When you spend time with your family members, do you listen when one of them speaks to you? Too often in today's fast-paced world we converse with others without even looking at them, even when they are sitting right across from us. Try this: The next time a family member talks to you, stop whatever you are doing and look directly at him or her. Stop texting, turn away from the computer, mute the television, or lay aside whatever else might distract you from listening. One of the best ways you can encourage your family and loved ones is to listen to what they are saying and then give them a response that reinforces the fact that you are listening.

- When you leave your house, take a look around at your neighbors' homes. If one of your neighbors is outside, stop and share a conversation with him. People are often encouraged just to know that someone has recognized them. If you don't have time to stop and talk, then at least wave and say hello. There are people, perhaps even among your neighbors, who wonder if anyone notices them at all.

- An encourager can often tell if someone has been crying or is angry, upset, or tired. To be an encourager, respond to a discouraged person by asking him or her if everything is OK or by inquiring as to how you can help. You may want to stay attentive to them through the course of the day, and then if you think they need further encouragement, approach them again with gentle dialogue.

Respond to those around you.

- Open the door for someone. Smile as you do it and say, "You first!"

- Let someone into the elevator before you, even if there's room for only one more.

- Offer to help carry the load that is too heavy for one person to handle.

- Tell someone at work that they've done a good job.

- Say thank you to cashiers, bank tellers, and restaurant servers.

- Write an extra note of thanks on the bottom of your bill. Be sure to include the first name of the person you're thanking and what they specifically did that you appreciate.

- Say thank you to the housekeeping staff at work. Learn their names too!

- Take time to call people you haven't seen in a while. Let them know you've missed them.

Invest your time and make a commitment.

- When you are home with your family, commit to spend uninterrupted time together at least once a week. Plan a game night or something interactive.

- If you have children involved in after-school sports, make time to go not only to their games but also to their practices as well. If you transport them, turn off your CDs or the radio and spend the travel time talking with them about what is important to them.

- Take time to celebrate birthdays with your coworkers. In addition to wishing them a happy birthday, have everybody in the office sign a card in which they write something that they admire about the person. What an incredible encouragement that would be!

- If there are staff members at your job who have been assigned a project requiring extra work or overtime, ask if there's anything you can do to help. If not, let them know you recognize and respect the hard work that has been demonstrated through everyone's commitment.

- If you have time to invest long-term, the best way to get involved in your community is through volunteerism. There are many local charities that could use some encouragement through your willingness to plug in wherever there is a need. Your involvement will spark a new level of enthusiasm among those who work at the charity as well as among the people the charity serves. It will be an encouraging win-win for everybody!

Chapter 3

Being a Connector

Let everything you say be good and helpful, so that your words will be an encouragement to those who hear them.
Ephesians 4:29

CONNECTORS ARE NATURALLY gifted in making people feel good. Their impact on someone's life may come during a chance meeting that lasts for one moment or through the development of a relationship that lasts a lifetime. In every case connectors understand the value of people and almost instantaneously create bonds that reach people's hearts.

Connectors see each person they meet as unique, and they instinctively want to tie into people's lives through meaningful words or actions. Picture an old-fashioned quilting bee where individuals bring their finely crafted masterpieces to be intricately stitched together with other unique yet exquisite works of art. In this case the connector is the one who understands that every square is an expression of the heart, mind, and soul of its individual artist.

From a connector's own perspective he is like the thread used to sew together each piece of the quilt with meticulous precision. The connector ensures that each piece reflects both the value of the individual contribution and the immeasurable worth of the finished product. That is, connectors see both the value of each individual as well as the significance of that person's role within the larger picture of serving others.

Connectors are very intuitive. They are able to immediately understand people and respond to them in ways that will draw them like a magnet. Teachers are often great connectors. They can be experts at seeing the possibilities in the lives of their students and at creatively guiding them to reach their full potential. The impact that teachers have on the hearts and minds of their students is astounding.

Connector teachers will always choose to influence students in ways that build up their core character and cause them to believe they have the ability to achieve their dreams. A teacher who is a connector will know how to reinforce the drive in each student in order to keep his hopes alive.

A connector teacher may sometimes have to create a systematic, long-term strategy to instill positive goals and healthy attitudes in his students. The following illustration shows how fragile a child's mind can be and how a connector teacher can turn a negative into a positive.

Every Child Is a Winner!

My first teaching job out of college was as an elementary school physical education teacher at a private school in Louisiana. During my first week on the job a little girl in the second grade approached me and asked, "Coach, are we going to have a field day this year?" I knew that having a field day was part of my contract, but it was only the third week in August, and the field day event was not scheduled until the following May!

I answered and said, "Oh yes, we will definitely be having a field day, but it will be a long time before May gets here. Why, you will almost be finished with the second grade by then."

"Well," the little girl sighed, "I already know I won't be going."

I looked at her with a puzzled expression and asked, "Why wouldn't you want to be part the field day?"

She replied, "I don't need to go. I already know I'm a loser."

Hearing that child's words sent a bone-chilling sensation throughout my body. As this little girl was only seven years old and already convinced she was a loser, I knew I had my work cut out for me. I promised God that day that as long as I had the privilege of teaching children, I would do everything in my power to build self-esteem into each student, no matter the child's skill level or athletic prowess. I pleaded with God to never let any of my students leave my classes thinking they were losers. Still green behind the ears in my teaching career yet so full of energy to change the world, I began to build a strategy for making critical changes to the curriculum for all grade levels.

My job as a connector teacher was to inspire each student individually to believe in himself. Since I saw five hundred students during the course of a day, I was challenged to create innovative ways of accomplishing my lofty goal. I wanted each student to not worry about their physical abilities or dwell on winning or losing games, so I created a curriculum based on the dynamics of movement and skill development. This took the pressure off the children who felt intimidated by the natural athletes in the class and created a level playing field.

The curriculum focused on station work rather than on playing an actual game in which there were winning and losing teams. I set up a circuit where students could rotate from one station to the other and where I could observe the members of each class on a much smaller scale. I was able to see each student experience success by prescribing skill-development techniques that each one could handle.

In addition to the station work I created movement routines choreographed to music in which the children worked on skill development by utilizing different pieces of equipment. This allowed them to synchronize with the rhythm of the songs and feel successful while handling equipment they may have initially feared. The individualized play curriculum took extensive time to develop, but the benefit to the children's confidence was monumental.

I saw myself as a connector teacher whose job was to inspire each child to see limitless possibilities before them and to never, ever define themselves as losers. Oh, by the way, for that first field day I held in May, I created a program titled "Everybody Wins," and my little second-grader was more than eager to attend. At the conclusion of the event her smile and her hug were enough encouragement to assure me that she had finally been set free from believing she was a loser and had become confident that the world held limitless possibilities for her.

This is one reason connectors feel right at home with groups of at-risk kids. They know they have the potential to inspire and motivate these precious children. Connectors realize that the more consistency and reliability they can demonstrate to the children, the greater the chances the little ones will open up their hearts and let them in. Below is a story about a special young man who allowed me to connect to his world of rebellion and isolation and was finally able to give me his trust.

Connecting to Leroy

Have you ever been in the right place at the perfect time to change a life? That is what happened to me one summer in Louisiana. While enjoying my summer break from teaching, I received a call from a fellow teacher asking for my help. As it turned out, there was a special children's reading program in desperate need of another instructor. My friend told me that the program had only one more week before completion, and because she did such a great job of convincing me that I would be meeting a huge need, I said yes.

The next morning I made my way into one of the poorest sections of our city in the hope that I could teach young children to be better readers. That same morning there was a little boy at the neighborhood reading program who absolutely did not want to be there another day. He had been miserable throughout the program and had convinced himself that this particular day would definitely be his last.

When I arrived at the community center, I met the head teacher, who explained the program and the reading curriculum we would be using that day. When I asked how I could help, she told me that she would like me to assist her with a little boy named Leroy. At that moment the door opened, and several students entered the room. One young boy sat down with a plop, slammed his books on the table, folded his arms, and stared into space with a look that definitely said he did not want to be there.

The head teacher looked at me and said, "That's Leroy!" She and I immediately walked over to him, and the teacher told him that it would have to be his last day if he continued to misbehave. Leroy shrugged his shoulders and looked at me with almost gleeful anticipation of his early exit from the program.

I introduced myself. I let Leroy know that I was glad he was there and that I was looking forward to helping him with the reading and spelling assignments for the day. He immediately responded that he already knew how to read and didn't want my help. So I asked, "Well, what do you want today?"

"I just want to go home," he replied.

I immediately bent down to his level and looked him straight in the eyes. "If you go home," I told him, "I will be really sad."

His only response was, "Why?" I shared with Leroy that I was excited to have him as a new friend and wanted to spend the morning with him. If he had to leave, I said, I would miss getting to know him.

Leroy looked as if he really didn't trust me or believe what I was saying, but he agreed to give our time together a try. All morning Leroy tried to make me angry, but I was determined to stay on task and provide a consistent response to his antics. At one point he pulled a chair out from under me, and at another he poked me with his pencil. My reactions stayed the same as Leroy kept testing me. Each time he misbehaved, I gave him correction. Then I would always say the same thing: "Leroy, I don't know why you want to hurt me, but I forgive you, and I love being here with you."

Leroy continued to test my patience, but I remained unwavering. Before he knew it, he had survived the day and had not been sent home! Now it was time for the kids to line up and head home, and in my heart I was celebrating. I knew that the rest of the staff had given up on little Leroy before he had even gotten to class that day, but God had not. He had put me in the right place at the right time with the right temperament to deliver the message of love and make a connection with this special little guy.

As the students departed, I gave each of them a nice big hug. When it was Leroy's turn, I hugged him and then squatted down to look again into his eyes so he could see my sincerity. I told him that I had loved being with him and couldn't wait to see him in the morning. Once again he looked at me like he didn't believe me. But sure enough the next morning he was one of the first students to arrive. He still darted in and slammed his books on the table, but this time he did not fold his arms or stare into space. Instead, he waved and looked right at me. I knew this was a positive sign that a connection was indeed in the works.

Over the next few days Leroy and I worked very hard on his reading skills and on his behavior. At the end of each day I gave Leroy his special hug, even if he didn't want one. I also made sure I told him that I loved him and looked forward to seeing him the next morning. By the last day of class Leroy had learned many new words and was actually having fun working through the reading activities.

When the children were dismissed, they all hurried out the door. I had been distracted with some sudden cleanup following a spilled drink, so I did not make it to the door in time to give each of the children a hug. I had to wave good-bye to them from a distance as they departed for the day.

Not long after the children had gone, I heard the door open, and someone came back into the room. I looked up from the desk I was cleaning and said, "Oh, hi, Leroy, did you forget something?"

Leroy bowed his head and shyly answered, "Yes, I came back for my hug."

I quickly ran over to Leroy and gave him what I am sure was the biggest hug he'd had in his whole life. And for the first time Leroy hugged me back. I knew at that moment that the protective barrier surrounding his heart was gone. I immediately said, "I love you, Leroy," and without hesitation, he replied, "I love you too."

He also told me that he was sorry for misbehaving and for hurting me with his pencil the first day we had worked together. I replied to Leroy with the gentle words, "I forgive you, Leroy, and I love you." I shared with him that I loved him not for the things that he did or didn't do but because of who he was. He was Leroy, and he was special. Leroy learned a new meaning for the word *love* that week. He knew in his heart what it felt like to be loved and to love back. He also knew that love went even deeper than the warm hugs from me.

Leroy and I spent more days together over the next few years, and when I had to move from Louisiana, I promised him that I would never forget him. I hope he finds out some day, perhaps maybe from this story, that indeed a lifelong connection with him was made in my heart that will remain there forever.

Connectors are gifted in being able to relate to people who are in need. In today's world of economic hard times there are more and more people in serious financial situations they've never experienced before. They are struggling to put food on the dinner table, pay their bills on time, and have enough money left over to put gas in the car. The heartbreak of losing a job or a business can be a severe blow, but having to endure the loss of a home to a foreclosure on top of the other losses is catastrophic.

The shattered economic state of millions has plunged people into a depth of despair that is rapidly draining their reservoir of hope. Connectors are perceptive, sharp, and insightful and can create solutions for reaching out to people without injuring their esteem or intruding on their privacy. This hurting world needs more connectors who can intervene with an understanding heart and provide wise counsel. Here is an example of a heartfelt connection that delivered the message of value to one very special man I'll call Mr. Smith.

A "You First, Me Second" Connection

One time at a huge community dinner for four thousand people I sat next to an elderly man whose appearance was quite disheveled. It was apparent that he had fallen on hard times and perhaps did not have access to a place to bathe or clean up. I greeted Mr. Smith with a welcoming handshake, and he smiled with a toothless grin. I started a conversation with him and found out that, in fact, he was homeless and had heard about the dinner through one of the local outreach agencies. I was glad that he had made it to the event and that he was getting some nourishment. He seemed to have become accepting of his situation and talked about how he hoped that someday things would change.

At the end of the evening I saw Mr. Smith getting ready to leave and asked him if he had transportation and a place to stay. "No," he replied, but he told me that he would be OK and not to worry. I asked him to wait by the door, and I told him that I would be right back. I scurried over to a friend I knew who had a car as well as some community connections that could possibly provide Mr. Smith some help. My friend was just leaving, and he offered to take the homeless man with him.

I watched as the two of them left, and the next day I asked my friend what had happened to Mr. Smith. My friend had gotten Mr. Smith a hotel room for the night so he could get cleaned up and sleep in a real bed. My friend also told me that he had taken Mr. Smith out to breakfast that morning and then taken him to a shelter, where Mr. Smith was able to find a more permanent place to stay. My friend extended a "you first, me second" hand of trust to this gentleman in need, and for the time being Mr. Smith was off the streets and in a safe place. I'm hoping that wherever Mr. Smith might be today, he has good memories to remind him that this world really does have people who care.

Connectors have the wisdom to know how to communicate in sensitive situations. Anyone who has ever experienced pain, suffering, struggles, hurts, or circumstances that have left them vulnerable will appreciate knowing that a connector will not bombard them with advice that is not needed or offer quick, insincere fixes. People in need of help want to be among those who can recognize and understand what is happening below the surface of a situation. At the right time and place, connectors provide that unique level of care that conveys understanding and elicits empathy. This is an account of one such moment in time when care was both given and received.

Connecting at the Heart

I will never forget the time I was finally on the road to recovery after having suffered a life-threatening blood clot that had sidelined me for a short period of time. I was so glad to be back in the community and doing what I love: connecting with people. I attended a community event at which I was delivering goodie bags to children who lived in a nearby at-risk neighborhood. The bags contained things such as books, toys, candy, and other fun items for children. I spent time personally handing the bags to each of the children who had been patiently waiting a turn.

It was not long before I encountered a little girl who was sobbing, and I thought perhaps she was tired or wanting to go home. I asked the woman I thought was her mom if the little girl was feeling OK. It turned out that the woman was actually the little girl's aunt, and what she said to me will forever remain etched in my mind and sealed in my heart. She told me her niece was crying because she wanted her mom. "Oh," I said, "is her mom at home or at work?" The aunt replied, "No, her mom, my sister, died two weeks ago." I gasped and told her I was so sorry. I asked her how her sister had died. She replied, "She had a blood clot, and it instantly killed her."

Immediately I knelt down, swept that little girl into my arms, and held her in a tight embrace for a very long time. Somehow I wanted her to know that I truly understood her pain, and because she had just as tight a grip on me as I had on her, I was assured that she welcomed my embrace. I struggled with my own thoughts about why this little girl's mom had died and I hadn't. At times like those life just doesn't seem fair. What could I do besides make a heart connection? Nothing.

But to this little girl and to me, for that moment in time, it was more than enough.

The message connectors deliver to others is that every individual is important. Connectors intrinsically know how to link with people whose interests may be different than theirs to form a harmonious bond, even if it's only for a moment. They are experts in making "you first, me second" connections that are sure to touch hearts and bring about positive momentum in another person's life. Any connector in your midst will seize opportunities to show people appreciation and value with great enthusiasm.

More Than Just the Money

Not too long ago I visited the local branch of my bank. I had some questions about moving money from one account to another as well as some other complicated account issues. I waited in line, and when it was my turn to be helped, the teller extended me a friendly greeting accompanied by a warm, welcoming smile. Immediately I felt at home and that my business was appreciated. When I explained my intentions to the teller, she responded with a very clear plan of action as to how to accomplish my goals in the most efficient and effective manner.

I was impressed. During the time she and I worked through the banking processes, I told her about some of the financial struggles my loved ones were experiencing, and she immediately connected with me, telling me that she had also been in the very same shoes. She shared how finally getting a job and having a steady income had given her the peace of mind that everything would eventually get better.

Throughout each of my banking transactions during that visit, the teller reconfirmed what she was doing for me and made sure that my expectations were being met. At the end of our short time together I wanted to make a connecting memory for this special young lady. I told her how much her friendly service had meant to me and that I wanted to let her supervisor know what an excellent job she had done for me. I asked for the name of the supervisor, noted the address of the bank branch, and proceeded home to write a letter to her supervisor detailing the significance of this young woman's service to me.

I placed my carefully crafted words on official work letterhead so the supervisor would know I was in management myself and understood the importance of serving others with excellence. I made sure to copy the young teller on the letter so the supervisor would know that she would also be in receipt of the letter. I included a business card in case the supervisor wanted to know more from me about the superb job her employee had done. As a connector I had a few short minutes with that young teller that may have turned into a memory for her because of the additional step I took to create a deeper bond. I hope the letter to the woman's supervisor gained the teller some well-deserved recognition. I also hope the teller received the message that her friendly demeanor and efficient service were of a far greater value to me than our monetary transaction.

Connectors make others feel comfortable in any setting. This ability to put people at ease is essential at community events and projects, where there is direct interaction between those who are serving and those being served. In the midst of diversity, connectors consistently convey genuine acceptance toward all.

When social responsibilities lead a connector into at-risk communities that may look precarious and where people may appear unapproachable, she is quite comfortable. The connector will be able to look beyond any differences and link directly to people's heart. There may be times when a connector will be introduced to someone and immediately create a bond. Even if a relationship is not established from the meeting, there will be an instantaneous rapport.

A Welcomed Hug

I once attended an event at which hundreds of people struggling through economic hard times stood in line for hours, waiting for bags of groceries. I was part of the team that had acquired and delivered over one hundred thousand pounds of food for this special community event, which thousands of people had been expected to attend. The goal had been to give away bags of groceries, each family receiving enough food to carry them through a few days. I was amazed that morning when I arrived and actually saw how many people were in need of help. As a connector I immediately felt compelled to personally greet each person with a warm welcome, even if the circumstances of hardship and struggle had been the reasons for our chance encounter.

I walked down the line, greeting our "guests" with enthusiasm and appreciation for their patience as they waited for their groceries. I met single moms, married couples, large families with lots of children, and people with special needs. I cooed along with tiny babies and squatted down to console little children who didn't understand why the line wasn't moving fast enough. I listened to stories of the difficult times individuals were having in making ends meet, and I tried to encourage them with the hope that things were bound to get better soon.

I came to an elderly lady whose face told the story that she had more than likely lived through many years of hardship. As I had with the others, I reached out and shook her hand to thank her for coming and to wish her well. It was then that I was captivated by the sadness in her eyes. Immediately I knew that this woman's pain was perhaps far greater than even her hunger. I gave her a spontaneous hug, and she began to weep. She shared with me that it had been well over a year since anyone had given her a hug, and at that moment my heart melted, and I embraced her again. It was a memorable moment for both of us that remains to this very day, a vivid picture of people needing people, and extending care and compassion without saying a word. That is what connectors live for.

Living "You First, Me Second"

A connector really listens in order to build others up.

A connector is alert to hearing what someone else is saying, knowing that it is vital to making a connection with long-lasting impact. In the case of the little girl in second grade who said she was a loser, her words were piercing to me, as they would have been to anyone wanting to be a better connector.

Too many times when people hear someone using self-condemning words, they reply with comments such as, "Oh, you know you're not a loser," or, "You shouldn't think that or say things like that." For connectors people's words prompt them to actively pursue a deeper connection through which they can identify the core of a person's pain and respond to it in ways that will move the individual to develop a more positive self-image.

A connector looks for ways to make instant bonds.

You don't have to build long-term relationships in order to make an impact in someone's life. A connector will be able to create an instant link or point of connectivity with people. In a few of the stories in this chapter, the connection was made through words of kindness and hugs. Who knows if Leroy, the young girl who wanted her mom, or the woman waiting in line are still talking about our hugs, but I know I am!

So how long has it been since you gave someone a good old-fashioned hug? If you're not a natural "hugger," why not make it a goal to hug at least one person a week? I have family members who will only give me a shoulder when I go for the full embrace, but as long as they know the affection that I'm trying to extend, I'm OK with that!

Connectors capitalize on shared experiences.

I swept the little girl who wanted her mom into my arms because of the intensity of my understanding of her sudden loss. She, on the other hand, was grieving for her mom, probably missing the natural affection that a mother gives her child. In the very long embrace we shared, I was able to give her, at least for those moments, an outlet for her grief—a chance to hold onto, perhaps, the feeling of being loved. It created a memory for me, and I have a feeling it did for her as well.

If you know someone who has experienced a difficulty that you've also been through, try making a connection with him or her. It doesn't have to be with a dramatic hug, but it can be through a conversation in which you offer that person an outlet for any grief, frustration, anger, or other emotion that may be pent up inside. Connectors can provide a safe environment for someone to download whatever lays heavy on his heart.

Connectors look for common interests.

The connection I made with the bank teller was initiated through a common topic of interest: economic hard times. The moment of connection happened when I first verbalized my satisfaction with her customer service and then was reemphasized when I told her I would notify her supervisor that she excelled at her job. The teller was not experiencing financial hardship herself, but she had in her past, and our shared experience was the stepping-stone to our connection. As humans we all need affirmation. Connectors are the best at finding the common link between people and making memories that instill value into people from every walk of life.

What places do you visit frequently? Connectors learn the names of those who provide them customer service and often engage in conversations with these people while they are being served. Try starting a conversation with a bank teller the next time you're at the bank or with the person at the post office who helps you mail your packages. What about with the postman who delivers your mail? The opportunities to connect with others are innumerable. Try making that first link, and then watch how the connection unfolds.

Connectors use their network to provide extended help to others.

Finally, in the story about the homeless man, I was able to gather information about his situation through a short conversation at a dinner table. Connectors not only connect in conversation, but if a person's need goes beyond the moment, they also use their network to complete the connection. If you want to be ready to extend connections, the main thing to remember is that you need to stay alert to the circumstances around you. A connector may miss an opportunity to link with another person because of distractions. Distractions come in different forms.

First, if you are in a setting in which you know you will be connecting with people, turn off your phone or silence it. Recognize that when you are with people, it is time to focus on seeking a connector. If while at an event a person was pouring out his heart to you and you stopped him to answer your phone, what message do you think you'd send to that person?

Second, don't fear people whose appearance may be disconcerting to you. Recognize instead that you can still make a connection, if only to speak positive words to someone who may be in desperate need of your affirmation.

For everyone who wants to be a better connector, the world is waiting for you. Wherever you go, look for your opportunity to make a connection, and remember to do the following:

- Get out into this world and mingle with other people.
- Initiate conversations with those you encounter.

- Be available to expand a connection once it's made.

Watch what happens! You will be amazed when you see how people react once they know someone really cares!

Chapter 4

Being a Volunteer of Excellence

Since you excel in so many ways—in your faith, your gifted speakers, your knowledge, your enthusiasm, and your love for us—now I want you to excel also in this gracious act of giving.
2 Corinthians 8:7

EXCELLENCE IS PERSONIFIED when the giving of one's time, talents, and energy impacts a life for positive change. Serving others while making excellence your standard can improve community programs, uplift the hearts of individuals, strengthen the dynamics of families, and provide support for charity work around the world. Those who sacrificially give of themselves through community service projects are highly valued, because they make a difference in the lives of the people they serve. That is why volunteerism is the heartbeat of community service, and it is excellent volunteers who empower nonprofit organizations to make the greatest impact.

There are many ways to get involved in volunteer service. You could participate in local programs that help children in need; provide care for the elderly, sick, and disabled; or feed those who are hungry. Perhaps you are a dedicated teacher who can volunteer to do extra tutoring or a lay leader who has time to get involved in your church's community outreach efforts. You could serve your community on behalf of your business through employee service days, or you could volunteer with a nonprofit organization through one of its community-based programs. Some of you, when you see a need, make yourselves available, whether that means giving someone your seat on a crowded bus or saving a life by administering CPR.

Whatever you do, when your goal is to help create positive change in your community, excellence should always be your standard. When volunteer service in a structured setting is performed with excellence and with a "you first, me second" mind-set, three qualities will be reflected: professionalism, responsibility, and ongoing engagement with those you serve.

Being professional

Whenever you volunteer in your community, your dress should be appropriate to the environment in which you will be serving. You should present yourself at the check-in site with a handshake and any further introduction necessary. A name tag or some visible identification is also appropriate.

Taking responsibility

Before your day of service, you should be aware of any responsibilities expected of you. Reports or evaluations that need to be filled out may be part of the volunteer's responsibilities, and expectations should be clarified ahead of time. If you are to report somewhere at a specific time, it is vital that you arrive ahead of the assigned time.

Staying engaged

Finally, it is important that you remain engaged with those you are serving. Get to know the people you are there to help, and enjoy your time with them. You will make memories that will last a lifetime.

Whether you volunteer periodically or so often that you lose track of the number of hours you've invested, every moment you spend serving others has value and significance. Yet the quality of your volunteer service is just as important as the quantity. From one person volunteering for an afternoon at a local food bank to another dedicating his time to a long-term building project, every volunteer's commitment to bring about change is momentous. Also, the value of your volunteer time is just as significant whether you are serving one person or are part of a team effort.

If a life has been impacted because you extended kindness to someone or if by loving your neighbor you have given someone a memory that will last forever, then your investment has made a difference. The value of your volunteer contribution to helping your fellow man then becomes immeasurable.

Excellence Plus Confidence!

One time I was asked to be a volunteer tutor for a young man whom I will call Damian. When I met Damian, he was a tall, handsome young man in the tenth grade. Somehow Damian had fallen through the cracks during his formative years and had not mastered basic elementary math skills.

As a professionally trained educator I knew how to put together an excellent plan of action that would lead Damian to believe in himself and achieve something he had never thought possible. He and I spent many weeks together. I reinforced my confidence in him, telling him that he could make it if he convinced himself never to give up. We celebrated his successes together at every incremental level of achievement he attained, and as time passed, I had the privilege of watching Damian's self-assurance grow and his esteem soar to new heights.

The excellence I longed to see from him was not academic brilliance but a teachable heart and a willing mind. Damian had both, and as a result he changed his life's path. He no longer saw himself as someone who couldn't make it in life. Instead, he purposed in his heart to meet every future challenge he faced head-on and to conquer it.

Damian finally became comfortable enough with himself to know that if he needed help, he didn't have to be embarrassed to ask for it. The result of our time together taught both Damian and me an important math lesson: the investment of excellence plus confidence equals infinite possibilities!

Volunteerism is also a way for businesses to impact their local communities. Community investment is now considered a corporate social responsibility, and the trend of only checkbook philanthropy has become a thing of the past. Today companies are interested in building relationships with nonprofit organizations within their communities through donations of their resources, financial support, or employee volunteerism. Businesses often create strategic partnerships with local nonprofits to target specific community needs within their cities.

Within these partnerships nonprofit leaders should have both the community expertise and communication skills to ensure that the expectations of the partnership will be met.

When companies commit to having their employees volunteer for community-investment projects or events, they should first gain the assurance from their community partners that every detail of the plan of action will be completed with excellence. When businesses engage in community partnerships, it is the responsibility of the charity to be sure that every aspect of an event, from start to finish, will convey the quality embodied in the company's brand.

One of the best examples of a company that excels in the area of community investment is Wells Fargo Bank. By setting their goals and expectations at the highest level of excellence, Wells Fargo not only exemplifies a strong commitment to providing quality customer service but also offers a rich heritage of employee dedication through volunteer programs that help people in numerous ways.

Wells Fargo is a team-oriented company. Every one of their employees is considered a vital part of the community and is encouraged to become active in his or her own sphere of influence. Wells Fargo's employees are allowed time away from work to volunteer at local organizations, and the company considers this a line of business that produces excellence in their community investment practices. Wells Fargo intuitively nurtures the passion of its employees who are dedicated to serving others by continually offering them opportunities to impact communities for positive change.

These impassioned employee-volunteers soar far beyond their job descriptions to a level of outstanding service. Through her commitment to serving others, one woman I know has made a tremendous impact on both the company where she worked and the community where she lives. Her name is Holly Cleveland, and with help from employee volunteers she has catapulted Wells Fargo of Jacksonville, Florida, to a new height of distinction in the area of social responsibility. Let me share a little about this remarkable woman.

A "You First, Me Second" Example of Excellence

Holly Cleveland recently retired from her position as community affairs officer of the Social Responsibility Group at Wells Fargo Bank. Because of her tremendous work in the community she received the 2008 President's Call to Service Award. This special service award is given in recognition of Americans who demonstrate a commitment to their communities and who inspire others to get involved in volunteer service. Holly was being honored for her incredible work ethic and tireless loyalty to volunteerism in America.

What made it even more special is that President George W. Bush personally gave this award to Holly. His plane landed at the airport in Jacksonville, Florida, and at a ceremony held on the tarmac, President Bush congratulated Holly and presented her with the award. The day Holly received that award is one she will always treasure in her heart and one that Wells Fargo Bank will long remember as a significant milestone in their quest to fulfill their goals toward exemplifying social responsibility with excellence.

Holly's commitment to social responsibility is deeply rooted in her character. Those who have worked with her, myself included, know that Holly will consistently demonstrate integrity in the workplace and uprightness of character in her community service. The quality of her work is impeccable. Holly's style of leadership is inspirational as well. In her former position Holly led hundreds of employee volunteers during community events, and the loyalty, respect, and reliability they demonstrated were a clear reflection of Holly's influence. She has an extraordinary way of communicating with volunteers and is incredible in her dealings with team members.

For over a decade Holly spearheaded the planning and execution of one very special annual event celebrating both Thanksgiving and Christmas. This event is held at the same city park located in Jacksonville, Florida, and includes over 275 volunteers from Wells Fargo Bank as well as volunteers from Winn-Dixie stores and football players from the Jacksonville Jaguars. The festivities are held outside, and whether rain or shine volunteers will spend five to six hours working together to create a spectacular community event at which more than 2,500 people receive groceries and needed hygiene items.

Well in advance of the event day, Holly would start the ball rolling by e-mailing an announcement of the upcoming event to employees and asking for willing volunteers. Within just a few minutes Holly could count on hearing from dozens who wanted to participate. The response was so great that many times Holly had to close the volunteer registration before the event occurred. As a result of Holly's leadership, this was one of Wells Fargo Bank's hallmark community events.

Holly's desire to achieve maximum community impact was demonstrated throughout each phase of the event. Every volunteer trusted Holly's directives, and because of Holly's attention to detail each one knew exactly what to expect. In order for the volunteers to safely arrive at the event site as a team, they ride together on chartered buses. Because of the event's excellent reputation the bus company donated the use of the buses and the drivers' time in support.

Another company in Jacksonville not only donates the forklifts needed to unload the tractor-trailer loads of food, but the owner of the company also donates his time to operate one of the forklifts for the duration of the event. He begins his day as early as six in the morning, and he works until well after the sun goes down. Winn-Dixie, another company that cares about its community, delivers a tractor-trailer load of donated food to the event. Volunteers then unpack and sort the food and place it in grocery bags.

Holly's event timeline was extremely well structured. As the buses arrive at the park, each volunteer disembarks wearing a Wells Fargo T-shirt. The volunteers immediately proceed to a check-in table, where they receive their job assignments, station locations, and an instruction sheet. Included on the instruction sheet is a designated time for each volunteer to take a lunch break. In addition to the drinks included in the lunch provided by Wells Fargo, Holly would make sure that her volunteers had plenty of water, as some years the November temperatures in Florida have climbed into the eighties.

The volunteers gain a sense of team accomplishment as they assemble mounds of grocery bags to give away. Holly was never afraid to roll up her sleeves and jump right in beside them to lift, carry, and stack boxes of food. She would move from station to station, encouraging and inspiring her volunteers.

I think for the volunteers one of the most enjoyable aspects of the event is interacting with the people they serve. This is where a direct connection can be made between the giver and the receiver. The volunteers know they are tangibly touching people's lives as they give out the grocery bags or, even better, as they help carry the groceries for the elderly or others in need of assistance. In many cases volunteers will give hugs and share encouraging words with a smile.

The memories the volunteers take home with them, as tired and sore as they might feel, energize their hearts. They know that they truly have made a difference in their community. To Holly that has always been the true measure of success.

I've seen Holly press through to complete an event even in the pouring rain. One year when the day was almost over and the cleanup well under way, a torrential downpour occurred, and both of us wound up soaked to the bone. With our hair matted and our makeup long gone, we couldn't help but burst into laughter when we saw the local news channel's truck arrive with a reporter and a camera crew! Thank goodness the news team decided that it was raining too hard for them to interview us! As they drove away, Holly and I just looked at each other and continued to laugh, but inwardly we both breathed a sigh of relief!

At the event each year Holly included Santa and Mrs. Claus to greet the children. Two big chairs are set up on the park's stage. A local promotion company donates hand-painted murals of winter scenes as well as a sound system for continuously playing special holiday music. Each child has an opportunity to sit on Santa's lap and to make his or her own special requests. There are also special bags for each of the children filled with books, candy, toys, toothbrushes, toothpaste, and other children's items.

After the children leave the stage, you often would see Holly squatting down to look directly into the eyes of the little ones to tell them how glad she is that they came. More often than not, her special words would trigger a hug from the children, who knew that her words were sincere and delivered straight from her heart to theirs.

One special part of the event tugged on Holly's heart. For several years the mother of one of Holly's volunteers crocheted multicolored caps for the children who would attend the event. She carefully stitched each cap with the same love and devotion she had expressed for her own children and grand-children. This was an event tradition each year until this wonderful woman passed away.

Because of Holly's heart for the children and her dedication to her volunteers, Holly wanted to find a way to continue this woman's work. She gallantly took on the task of teaching herself to crochet. It wasn't long before Holly was producing crocheted caps by the dozen. Because of her inspiring example another employee joined Holly's venture, and together the two of them crocheted enough caps for all the children attending the event!

The caps have remained a tradition because Holly was driven to serve in every area with excellence, exerting every ounce of energy she had for the benefit of those in need. Indeed she is a role model for all business leaders who are committed to fulfilling their social-responsibility obligations through exceptional service for the benefit of community investment. Despite Holly's retirement her proven track record of excellence has become the standard for volunteers to emulate, and her "you first, me second" legacy will live on.

Living "You First, Me Second"

When excellence is the standard in volunteer service, it will have a powerful impact on a community. Those who work in the community relations or community affairs divisions of their companies will often be looking for volunteer organizations through which their employee volunteerism programs can most effectively be implemented.

There also are opportunities for individuals and professionals to plug their talents into volunteer service. Community-based organizations, charities, and other nonprofits often depend on volunteers. Because many of these organizations operate on a shoestring budget and therefore are often under-staffed, they can greatly benefit from people who have expertise and proficiency in a trade or profession. If you are available to volunteer your time and your talents, nonprofit organizations would welcome your services to help them fulfill their mission with excellence.

Charities and nonprofits often appreciate management and administrative guidance from professionals in those fields. Lending your support to one of these groups will strengthen the work of those community organizations as they strive to impact people in need. Wherever you can help, I am sure your services would be appreciated. However, your standard should be to demonstrate excellence, even though you are not being paid for your efforts. No one wants to redo work because it wasn't completed properly the first time. The volunteer community service you provide should represent the same kind of quality that you would give if you were being highly compensated.

Here are a few ideas to get you thinking about how your knowledge or specific trade could benefit nonprofit groups:

- If you have IT experience, your help is most likely desperately needed. With the limited availability of people who have expertise in this area, organizations lose hours and hours trying to solve technology problems through guess-work and hunches. In addition to fixing problems, IT experts can help create websites and donor databases as well as donation-tracking systems for warehousing and inventory control purposes.

- If you are skilled in general contracting, painting, or maintenance work, you could offer your services to help repair or restore a neglected area within the organization's office building, or you could freshen up a work space with a coat of paint. If you like working outdoors, there may be a need for trimming, edging, or mowing the grass.

- If you are an educator, you could offer suggestions for improving after-school programs or for tutoring at-risk children.

- If you have knowledge in the field of graphic arts, you could give guidance for creating thank-you pieces or designing logos and fact sheets.

- If you are skilled in journalism, you can be of great benefit to an organization's writing staff as they prepare information pieces as well as appeal letters going out to the organization's donor base.

- If your expertise is in the field of marketing, you could spend time looking at the organization's website, video clips, and picture libraries to help identify which media pieces best represent the passion behind the organization's mission.

- If you are a skilled administrator, your talents are often needed in helping with grant applications. Sometimes applying for grants can be a long and tedious process, and having someone with excellent language and grammar skills as well as superior typing skills can substantially ease the burden often experienced in the preparation of paperwork.

- If you are certified in counseling, volunteers are often needed to assist victims of disasters in coping with unexpected and substantial losses.

- If you are fluent in a foreign language and the charity has a global reach, your expertise may be needed in providing translation services.

I hope that this list has helped you start thinking about specific ways you could invest your talents, skills, and abilities in helping charities and community organizations whose mission is to reach out to people in need. If you have access to a computer and would like to find a charity or organization whose mission is a good fit for you, type the word "volunteer" into your search engine. You should see multiple links to the websites of volunteer agencies in your area. Also, if you are looking for a good review site for charities, a good source of information is www.charitynavigator.com.

Volunteering is the foundational component for maximum community impact. When you become aware of a need and are able to use your talents to meet that need, you will be hooked on all the benefits that volunteering has to offer. The satisfaction of knowing that you're making a difference is the impetus that will take you from being a neighborhood resident to a committed volunteer with a defined mission to change your world.

Chapter 5

Being Persistent

So let's not get tired of doing what is good. At just the right time we will reap a harvest of blessing if we don't give up.
Galatians 6:9

PERSISTENCE IS EMBEDDED inside those with rock-solid character. It is built on a determination to continue doing or trying something, even if it proves to be difficult. Persistent people are unwavering. They set their minds on staying the course, remaining steady and resolute until their goals are achieved. They possess a grit that drives them to achieve goals that others consider impossible. They live out the motto, "If you believe, you will persist." The key to this kind of persistence is being confident that you are equipped with everything it takes to be successful.

Persistent people are resilient, even in the face of obstacles. When they encounter setbacks, they bounce back with an even greater zeal to complete their mission and to finish it well. They have an incredible knack for remaining focused, giving them a distinct advantage over others, especially when the challenges of life occur without warning.

My mom was a persistent woman. She worked outside the home during the week and used her weekends to catch up on chores around the house. When she became a single mom, she was determined from the very beginning to make things work, no matter what. That included enduring the end of her marriage and an eviction from her apartment in which all of her household possessions were put on the front lawn.

The furniture with outstanding debt for nonpayment was repossessed by creditors, and the antiques that had been in her family for generations were hauled away for immediate storage. My mom chose not to share about what happened to those precious family items she watched being driven away that day, but none of us would ever see them again. For many years times were tough, but it was my mom's persistence that kept all of us believing there would be a better tomorrow.

Persistent people defy pessimism and do not allow negativity to weigh them down. They can see the light at the end of a tunnel when everyone else has given up. People who are persistent are wise when weighing the limitations of each project they face. They understand that timing is the key to knowing how far to push and how deep to dig in with their steadfast determination to conquer the impossible.

Persistent people are usually high achievers; however, they remain teachable because they know that the best learning comes through situations in which they will be stretched. Over time they develop a resilience that gives them the fortitude to plow through even the most complex challenges. Arising from this relentless pursuit to finish well are a dedication and a commitment that are unbending.

Persistent people are also well suited for creating partnerships for the benefit of others and greater community impact. When someone's goal is to accomplish something for the benefit of others, his persistence will always prevail. Below is a story that illustrates how persistence kept hope alive long enough for a dream to become a reality.

"You First, Me Second" Persistence

One day Bill Horan, the president of Operation Blessing, came into my office and gave me a handwritten note from his mother, Luella. Attached to her note was an article that she had read regarding an excessive amount of nonfat dry milk (NDM) that the government had been storing for a long time in underground facilities across multiple Midwestern states. The NDM had been accumulating in monumental proportions, and none of it was being used. In her note Luella asked, "Bill, would you please see if you can do something about this? Can't some of this milk be delivered to those who are hungry and cannot afford to buy it?"

Bill grinned as he watched me read his mother's note and then aptly replied, "Pam, please see if you can find someone in charge of this situation and let them know that we are equipped to help them solve this problem."

Bill knew that what he was asking of me was not an easy task. He had, however, grown up seeing his mother's persistence and determination. After his sister, Virginia, was born with Down syndrome, Bill saw Luella champion the cause of people with intellectual disabilities. With her endless supply of love for her daughter and her compassion for others Luella had been a tireless advocate for those in need for more than fifty years. Luella was an avid reader, and when she discovered the article about the excess milk powder, she confidently charged her son with making sure people in need received some help.

I took a deep breath and told Bill I would get on it right away. The article had mentioned the US Department of Agriculture (USDA), so I started there. Immediately I began making cold calls, and each one seemed to lead nowhere. It was almost two weeks to the day after I started my quest that I finally got the break I needed. After dozens of attempts to find someone who could help me, I was put in touch with the USDA division that had detailed information about the situation. A powerful relationship merger was made that day between me and two USDA employees: a man also named Bill and his coworker, Bea.

On my initial call I spoke only with Bill. I shared with him that we had a fleet of fifty-three-foot tractor-trailers that could help transport the milk powder from the storage areas to our network of nonprofit food agencies. I assured him that the NDM could be distributed directly to those who were experiencing hardship. I also told him that because we had our own dispatchers and drivers, our expert operational staff could easily manage the pickups and deliveries internally. Our staff understood complex transportation issues and was accustomed to working through logistical challenges.

It was not long into that first conversation that I learned the milk powder would not be released from storage quickly. Bill said a detailed plan of action had to be developed from scratch and that because this was the first time an allocation of this kind had been considered, the process could turn out to be a very lengthy one. Bill knew that more people had to be brought into the loop, and this is where I was introduced to Bea.

As the three of us discussed the situation, we agreed on a three-step plan of action. The first step would be to substantiate the need of releasing the NDM, the second would be to put accountability measures in place, and the third would be to map out the logistics of our proposal. Bea took on the primary role of leading the charge to transform the plan into a reality.

I remember the first time I met Bea face-to-face. It was a stormy night in the middle of the summer in Washington DC. We had agreed to have dinner together at a restaurant located halfway between her house and the location where I was bedding down for a few nights. By the time I arrived at the restaurant, thunder was clashing and bolts of lightning illuminated the evening sky. Once inside I immediately recognized Bea, even though we had talked only a few times on the phone. When I saw her smile, I knew it had to be her.

Bea and I spent hours in conversation over dinner and coffee that night. She shared with me her passion for people in America who were experiencing hunger and poverty. Her words were laced with compassion, yet she spoke with a sense of determination and urgency that something had to be done. Together, she said, we could bring hope to people who were struggling to make ends meet. The intensity of her words was compelling, and its impact on me that night was very telling. The more we talked, the clearer it became that she and I were about to embark on a huge undertaking. But persistent people are not scared away by hard work. On that stormy night we agreed that we were ready, willing, able, and up for the challenge.

As the plans unfolded, Bea's persistence became her compass. Over the next several months Bea labored tirelessly through mounds of paperwork, piles of memos, and stacks of research documents. She and I also spent hours learning about each other's worlds. When relationship mergers occur between two or more organizations that operate differently from one another (in this case, the US government and a non-profit charity), it is important to glean as much knowledge and understanding as possible about each other's work.

I carefully perused websites and links to more information about the USDA and its structure, programs, and departments. Bea, on the other hand, spent an equal amount of time studying the world of nonprofits and what motivates them to want to make a difference. She was curious to discover the different levels of responsibility involved in our regular distribution of food to thousands of hunger-relief agencies across the country, especially since we picked up and delivered more than one hundred million pounds of food per year! Bea and I continued to query each other about programs and policies so that our final USDA initiative would dovetail perfectly for all parties involved.

Bill, Bea, and I continued to work through every layer of accountability, and we found ourselves in an extensively detailed process requiring focus and creative thought. There were days when we felt like we were progressing at a turtle's pace, but we persisted over every hurdle. Many of the obstacles we faced probably would have caused anyone else to quit, but Bea and I remembered the commitment we had made at our dinner together that stormy summer night. After each setback we became more relentless in our pursuit to finish the task.

Finally our persistence paid off. More than a year after our first dinner together and after sitting in seemingly endless numbers of meetings, burning the midnight oil, and plowing through mounds of paperwork and bureaucratic red tape, it finally happened: the first government initiative of its kind was completed and sent to the secretary of agriculture for a signature. Not long after the project's completion, the secretary held an official press conference in Washington DC to launch the National Nonprofit Humanitarian Initiative (NNHI). Bill, Bea, and I were privileged to be part of the celebration and to see firsthand that our persistence had indeed paid off.

The milk powder was released to all nonprofit organizations across America that had hunger-relief programs. Every nonprofit that could use the milk powder within their distribution program was given the opportunity to fill out the application paperwork for donation requests. The program resulted in the release of more than forty million pounds of nonfat dry milk to be donated to all national and community nonprofit organizations that met the qualifications for distribution accountability.

The initiative could not have been a better solution for this problem that had seemed insurmountable. Not too many people know about the tremendous impact that resulted from Bea's efforts, but recognition is not what was most important to her. She simply found great satisfaction in knowing that her persistence had conquered every obstacle and that those she cared about most were finally receiving the help they so desperately needed.

Emerging from the milk powder distributions were incredible stories of how struggling families across the country were being helped, how babies who had been deprived of nourishment had returned to good health, and how nonprofits had been strengthened in their ability to demonstrate care for their communities. The outcome of an incredibly successful collaboration left an indelible memory in the hearts and minds of the workers in thousands of community organizations and of our friends in the USDA. Who would have thought a story with such an extraordinary ending could have started with a simple handwritten note from a mother urging her son to do something to make a difference!

Living "You First, Me Second"

Do you find that you sometimes get halfway through a project and then stop? The next thing you know, time has slipped away and you're unable to get the project started up again. Are there a lot of distractions in your life that keep you from seeing your plans through to completion? Rest assured that you are not alone. Many people find themselves jumping into projects with a great deal of enthusiasm and then, before they know it, more important tasks or time-consuming interruptions seem to crowd into their schedules, and the project invariably becomes an idea of the past. If you have wondered if there is any way you can improve your ability to complete tasks, there is! Below are a few suggestions:

1. Start with short-term acts of kindness.

   • Choose a project that you know you can complete in a short period of time.

   • Perhaps bake a batch of brownies or cookies for the local fire department. Then deliver it to the firefighters with a big smile and a "thanks." After you deliver the goodies, reflect on how you feel. Was the experience positive enough to make you want to do something else? If you can embrace the inward satisfaction of having completed a kind act for the benefit of others, you will lay the foundation for building your strength of mind and determination to persist with tasks in the future.

• Look at the needs right in your own neighborhood. See if you can find a home in which a person lives alone or an elderly couple who spends most of their time inside or an individual with a family member who is battling cancer or another long-term illness. Now take a look at the outside of the home. Does the yard need weeds pulled, grass mowed, or shrubs trimmed? If so, then put yourself in charge of gathering a group of friends together to spend a few hours doing some yard work and cleanup. What may have seemed an overwhelming task to the family living inside will now become a met need that can encourage their hearts and send the message that someone cares about them—not to mention that it will enhance their home's curb appeal. By accomplishing random acts of kindness, you will tangibly live out the command to "love your neighbor." Can you think of other projects that can benefit others that you could complete in a relatively small amount of time?

2. Increase your commitment by involving yourself in community work for a full day.

- Clear your calendar—no excuses. Be prepared ahead of time, putting all the arrangements in place so you can look forward to your day of service.

- Choose a project you enjoy so you have fun while you are helping others. After the day is over, reflect on how you felt while in the midst of making a difference in someone else's life. See if you can schedule a few more one-day commitments during the next month or so. Through these experiences you will not only help others, but you will also build persistence into your character in manageable pieces.

3. As you prepare for making longer commitments to serving others, enlist a friend to commit to being an accountability partner for you.

- Choose a friend you can trust and whom you enjoy being around—someone who will hold you to your commitment without making you feel resentful.

- You need to be open to some possible nudging, prodding, or even forceful reminders that others are counting on you.

- Make sure your commitment to your task is manageable so that you remain diligent until its completion.

4. Once you have a few projects and special acts of service completed, try expanding your

commitment to see a project through from start to finish. For example:

- Tutor a student for an entire semester.

- Volunteer to be a teacher's aide at your local school.

- Coach a local youth basketball team.

- Work at the local food pantry and help buy, pack, and deliver groceries for those in need.

- Offer to be a volunteer grant writer for a local nonprofit organization. Make it your goal to keep asking until you finally get a positive response and grant money comes into the organization.

You may not have the opportunity I had to help write a government initiative, but you can be a vital part of making a difference in the lives of other people. When your confidence grows and you see yourself following a task through to completion, the people you serve will drive you to persist. The more you seek to extend your willingness to help others, the more opportunities you will find. As you increase your commitment to serve with a "you first, me second" persistence, you will see lives changed because of your personal investment to stay the course and not give up.

Chapter 6

Being Dedicated

*But Ruth replied, "Don't ask me to leave you and turn back.
Wherever you go, I will go; wherever you live, I will live. Your
people will be my people, and your God will be my God."*
Ruth 1:16

DEDICATION INVOLVES A commitment from deep
within your very being. When dedication is activated
for the benefit of others, it becomes rich with purpose.

A deeply rooted commitment to serve others is evident
in many professions. We see it in firemen who are dedicated
to rescuing people from potential catastrophic conditions, in
nurses who are committed to providing not only needed health
care but also an extra measure of compassion, in teachers who
are loyal to instructing children to give them the promise of
a better future, in pastors who are faithful to shepherd their
congregations through life's issues, in policemen who risk their
lives to fulfill their call of duty, and in soldiers who commit to
serving their country and protecting its citizens.

The work these people do is not for the money. It's not for the fame. It's not for the power or the prestige. It is for the privilege of serving.

Dedicated people have setbacks, challenges, hardships, and even tragedies in life, but these experiences are actually the fertile soil in which dedication takes root. People who have conquered adversity will agree that dedication to finish what you started, even through difficulties, generates a deep satisfaction within the soul.

Dedicated community heroes are all around us, taking care of people in need. There are many servants who have devoted hearts and determined minds to remain steadfast in their service for the benefit of others. Some keep serving in the midst of huge struggles and setbacks. It is my honor to highlight two genuine community heroes and one successful businessman. All of them have kept their devotion alive despite having had to conquer more than their share of obstacles.

Allegiance and Devotion

Donnie and her husband, Joe, own a local florist shop. Donnie and Joe were the perfect picture of a couple committed to each other, to the success of their business, and to serving their community. A few years ago, however, Joe was diagnosed with cancer, and it was then that both of their lives took a different turn.

All who have suffered from cancer or who know someone who has battled the disease are very aware of the long, sometimes lonely road that may or may not lead to full recovery. During the course of Joe's battle there were surgeries, hospitalizations, and a variety of ongoing treatments. Throughout all his care management and the related side effects, Joe continued to faithfully deliver his bouquets of flowers and beautiful floral arrangements with a smile and a heartfelt hello to the people in his community.

Joe bravely fought through every setback with Donnie right by his side, but he eventually lost his battle and passed away. Donnie, now on her own, finds comfort in being able to continue serving others at the floral shop that she and Joe built together. She provides her customers with service beyond their expectations, faithfully preparing beautiful arrangements each day with the hope that people will be encouraged and heavy hearts will be lifted.

Because of Donnie's dedicated service, many of her regular customers would unequivocally call her a friend. Recently I stopped by Donnie's shop to pick up a gift certificate she was donating as a door prize for a special community event. Her desire was to bless other people the way so many had blessed her, especially during the difficult times she and Joe had endured. I think everyone who knows Donnie would agree that she is indeed her own bouquet of sunshine.

Dedicated people are not afraid of hard work, nor are they fearful of their own ambitions or dreams. People with dedication have constancy within that provides the needed staying power for them to remain steadfast and resolute. Those who are dedicated innately know how to keep a dream alive without losing hope and how to diligently work toward a goal without losing heart. They can commit wholeheartedly to completing a task, and the key to their success is focused ambition and determination.

Perseverance and
Dogged Determination

Ask Bob Howorka from Murray, Kentucky, about what is important to him, and he will tell you that there is no greater satisfaction than what he does every day of his life: serving his community. Bob and his wife, Allison, retired in 1993 after working in management positions for the Sears Corporation in Minneapolis, Minnesota. After retiring, they decided to move to Charleston, South Carolina, where they started working in real estate development.

Bob and Allison became active in their church and in their community, but both of them sensed that they wanted to do more. It was not too long before they started a nonprofit organization offering a variety of programs for the community such as GED classes, life skills, a variety of children's programs, and a hunger-relief feeding program.

With their dedication propelling them full-speed ahead, Bob and Allison felt unstoppable. That is, until doctors discovered cancer in Bob's lymph nodes. Calling upon the same dedication with which he approached life, Bob began his relentless battle through long, agonizing months of chemotherapy treatments. In the midst of Bob's battle he and Allison decided to move back to Allison's hometown of Murray, Kentucky, where Bob continued his treatments to their completion and worked on regaining his strength.

It wasn't long after settling into Murray that Bob and Allison resumed their community nonprofit work. This time their main focus would be on hunger-relief efforts for families in need of help. Initially the couple rented a space at an abandoned grocery store. They opened their doors for business, and

Bob and Allison depended on a dedicated staff (all of whom were volunteers) to help unload and sort food that was regularly delivered by tractor-trailers.

In no time the number of community organizations throughout the county receiving food through Bob and Allison's nonprofit grew to over twenty-five. Bob and Allison moved their operations to another warehousing facility. Since their arrival in Murray more than 4.5 million pounds of food have been distributed through their organization.

Unfortunately Bob's cancer has returned, but he is determined to stay on course with the food-distribution program as he fights through more chemotherapy treatments. Serving people is Bob's life's passion, and the dedication he has demonstrated through his ups and downs is remarkable. Bob would be quick to give credit to his extraordinary group of volunteers, who are his inspiration. They have been dedicated from the beginning to assist Bob every month like clockwork.

Allison continues to be Bob's faithful helper, keeping the nonprofit's operations and paperwork current. Her responsibilities have been increasing, however, since Bob started fighting a progressive loss of vision caused by macular degeneration. In the midst of all these challenges Bob and Allison's dedication to serve is unparalleled. If you met this fabulous couple, you would never believe that Bob is eighty years old. With his zeal for living, he would be the first to tell you to step aside—he's just now getting his second wind!

"You First, Me Second"
Dedication Beyond Borders

I've met very few business leaders whose commitment to making a difference contributes as dynamically to their character as Mr. Paul Heiman's does. Mr. Heiman is the patriarch of the family-owned company Standard Textile, a global textile manufacturing company headquartered in Cincinnati, Ohio. Mr. Heiman's generosity in caring for people extends to countries far beyond our US borders. His dedication serves the poorest of the poor, from those living in humble surroundings in densely populated cities to people residing in small villages in very remote regions of the world.

From his bounty Mr. Heiman freely gives products manufactured by his company to nonprofit organizations that work with impoverished communities around the globe. Some of his product donations include hospital gowns, blankets, sheets, pillowcases, operating room drapes, scrubs, baby blankets, and crib sheets. These textiles are shipped to various countries so that hospitals and clinics can be better equipped to provide care for the neediest populations throughout the world.

Mr. Heiman is also dedicated to serving his family, his employees, and his community. Being a Holocaust survivor, Mr. Heiman knows what it means to live in uncertainty. His experience in struggling through immense obstacles is what makes him who he is today: a man dedicated from his heart to helping people. One of those people is a baby girl who lives in a remote village far, far away from Cincinnati, Ohio. Mr. Heiman's act of kindness toward her has made a profound and long-lasting impact in the life of this little girl named Belkis, whose family lives in Honduras. Belkis's life was impacted because Mr. Heiman's instinctively responded to an urgent plea for help.

When Belkis was five months old, she suffered second-degree burns as a result of an accident that occurred in the backyard of her parents' home located in a remote village in Comayagua, Honduras. Her mother had started a fire to heat a pot of water, and without warning Belkis's two-year-old sister grabbed one of the sticks from the fire and accidentally ignited the hammock in which Belkis was sleeping.

Belkis's mother ran to her baby and grabbed her from the burning hammock, but not before Belkis had sustained major burns to her forehead and scalp. Despite her panic Belkis's mother was able to cover the baby's little head for protection, but she knew she had to get medical help to save her baby girl's life.

From their village it took three hours to reach the nearest bus stop. Belkis's mother wrapped her baby securely in her arms and set out on the long journey with a relentless determination propelled only by the love of a mother for her child. Once on the bus it was another two hours before they arrived in Tegucigalpa, the capital city of Honduras, where Belkis could finally be seen by a doctor.

In Tegucigalpa there is a pediatric burn rehabilitation center equipped with a brightly colored room, rehabilitative equipment designed for children, and a variety of activity stations. The founder of the center had been a burn victim himself after surviving a 1989 plane crash. The nonprofit center offers free medical services to children from all over Honduras and is funded through individual contributions.

The center is equipped with sewing machines, and volunteer seamstresses make every garment worn by the children who are being treated for burns. The quality of the thread used to stitch each garment contributes directly to the healing process of the children's wounds. By producing the perfect amount of pressure on the burn, the garments that are made with this thread ensure that a wound will not worsen, especially when bandages have to be changed. It was after Belkis arrived at the center that I was contacted with the news that the center had run out of their highest-quality thread.

Without hesitation I called Doris, who works for Mr. Heiman, in hopes that Standard Textile had the kind of thread the burn center needed. To my dismay she said they did not manufacture the special thread; however, she said Mr. Heiman knew who did. I suddenly felt as if a ray of hope had shined down upon us. Mr. Heiman made a phone call to the thread supplier and ordered exactly what was needed for little Belkis's injuries. I was assured that the thread would be shipped right away, and in a very short time, the thread was in the hands of the burn center's dedicated seamstresses.

When Belkis arrived at the center, her tiny head was covered with the necessary ointments and medications, and a burn garment was placed over her wounds until the special thread arrived. It was not long before the seamstresses were able to make Belkis's special garment that would better protect the sensitive burns on her little head. Because Mr. Heiman embraced this situation with a relentless dedication, the cap Belkis needed for maximum healing was stitched just in time!

When a relationship merger is wrapped in dedication, each partner involved goes the extra mile in support of the other. Mr. Heiman did not have to order the thread for little Belkis's cap. He could have said that he was sorry he didn't have what was needed and ended the call. But instead he made it his mission to provide the help that Belkis so desperately needed. Mr. Heiman demonstrated his dedication by truly living out to the fullest extent the adage "You can count on me!" Belkis is still too young to express her gratitude to Mr. Heiman, but the depth of her mother's appreciation is definitely captured through the twinkle in her eyes and the genuine sincerity in her most grateful smile.

Mr. Heiman is a leader dedicated to serving people around the globe and to helping break their cycles of suffering. His focus on people's needs is making a difference in many lives, and because of his generous donations of medical textiles, tens of thousands of people around the world have received his special messages of devoted care. His dedication to community investment is making a global impact, one precious life at a time.

There is nothing more satisfying than being in a relationship with people who are not only committed to the work they do but who also are dedicated wholeheartedly to the people they serve. What makes our alliance with Mr. Heiman and Standard Textile so special is that it is rooted in authenticity and built on a solid foundation of trust.

Living "You First, Me Second"

The kind of dedication described throughout this chapter comes from deep within a person's soul and communicates genuine concern because it is generated from the heart. Your "you first, me second" devotion will be activated when you live to build up and bless others rather than yourself.

When building the quality of dedication in your life, the best way to get started is to honor someone through the investment of your time. This person may be a loved one, or it could be someone who has passed away whose memory you hope to honor. Or it may be someone you would like to honor because the person has overcome or achieved something, or has survived a difficult circumstance. When you begin to build the quality of dedication, start with the familiar. Below are a few suggestions that may be of help:

- One of my coworkers has a child with special needs. This man has dedicated his time outside the office to supporting local and national events that build awareness of special needs and that fund the research that he hopes will make a difference in the future. My coworker's service in the community honors his son, and his dedication to these efforts is evident to all.

- You may have a loved one or a personal friend who has lived through and survived domestic abuse. You could dedicate your time and service to help support a local women's shelter. The drive in you will be precipitated by the dedication you have to make a difference so others will be spared the kind of pain your loved one endured.

- Perhaps you have within your extended family a child who has been diagnosed with a crippling disease. If there are no support groups in your area for people who have this disease, your dedication to making a difference can be activated, and you can become driven to start a support group yourself. Begin by putting together a discussion group within your circle of friends and create a plan of action for how to move forward.

- Maybe you have adopted children. The dedication in you that knows and understands the incredible love you have for your child may lead you to sponsor a child who lives in a third world country. If your adopted child is old enough, let him be a part of the sponsorship process with you. Your devotion will become a tangible demonstration to those around you and may spur others on to sponsor children as well.

- You may have a loved one or a friend who has lost his or her life in service to their country. You may have an opportunity to give back in honor of this person by dedicating your time to help returning veterans find jobs. Or perhaps you can offer wounded veterans the compassion that will let them know that someone cares. Or maybe you can get involved in sending care packages to our servicemen and women who are still serving overseas. This dedicated service in honor of your loved one ultimately blesses others.

The list has no end, because there are as many ways to dedicate your time and service as there are people you can honor. Numerous support groups, charities, and organizations that target health and social issues are already in existence, and researching them on the Internet will help you find exactly the right fit for you. The important thing to remember when you are serving on behalf of someone else is the person in your life who is motivating you to dedicate your service. Dedication is rooted in loyalty and allegiance. Your purpose will become defined as your devotion grows into a compelling drive within you to make a difference on behalf of someone else.

As you dedicate your time and service to reach out to others, the affection you have for your loved one will leave an indelible signature on the hearts and minds of those you touch. Do you know where you will leave your mark?

Chapter 7

Being Passionate

Love each other deeply with all your heart.
1 Peter 1:22

I F I WERE to describe myself in relation to the work I do, I would say that I am passionate. From the time I was hired by Operation Blessing in 1995, I knew that this was destined to be more than just a job. My passion is the underlying reason I've spent nearly two decades pleading the cause of the poor and needy, and not once has it felt like work.

My primary responsibility at work is to acquire donated products to give to those who are suffering or have fallen on hard times, those who are hungry or in urgent need of life-saving medicine, or those who are the victims of natural and man-made disasters. My life and work are the heartbeat of my purpose, and the relentless energy that keeps me focused and driven comes from the passion within me for the millions of people I have the privilege of serving.

Passion is fervor that stays focused and directed. It is not about doing; it is about being. Passion is the why behind what you do. I began to nurture passion for what I do after I personally embraced the calling to become an advocate for people in need, especially those caught in the perilous cycle of suffering. Every day I'm gripped with an urgency to connect with businesses that have the resources to help others.

One of my daily tasks is to approach companies and ask for donations to help meet the needs of people all over the world. Many times I am told no, but because of my passion I keep searching for the needed resources. I am compelled to help those who depend on these kinds of provisions to sustain them, and it's my passion that keeps me asking, even if I am told nothing is available.

With passion you become committed to staying the course. When you are fueled by passion, you will be able to blaze through challenges and conquer mountains of adversity in order to produce positive and effective change. Passion is a powerful and compelling emotion. It comes from within the deepest parts of our inmost being, and when it is combined with purpose, it becomes a powerful, life-transforming force propelling us forward. When I think of this kind of passion, a woman who immediately comes to mind is B. J. Waymer, one of the finest leaders in the field of community investment.

The owner of B. J. Waymer Associates, Inc., a boutique cause-marketing and communications firm based in North Carolina, BJ designs and implements corporate special events in local and national markets. Whether it is communicating the philanthropic goals of a corporation or translating the special interests of its sponsors, BJ's job is to build impactful outreach programs that meet the needs of target audiences and engage fragile communities. BJ's specialty is the creation of unique, impactful, and sustainable programming.

She is an expert in developing strategic alliances with businesses, communities, governments, and nonprofit leaders to assess need, harness resources, and implement programs that make a marked difference in the lives of her clients' target audiences—children, small business owners, and nonprofits. Waymer Associates' primary client is the National Football League. BJ serves as a strategic consultant for NFL Charities and the NFL Player Care Foundation, and she is a special project producer for the NFL's marketing and community relations departments for both Super Bowl and Pro Bowl events.

BJ produces the league's Play 60 Pro Bowl Youth Fitness Clinics each year, utilizing the entire roster of Pro Bowl players and serving five hundred-plus students in one day. She developed the NFL's long-running Small Business Leadership Forum and Workshop series and was instrumental in the creation of One World, an in-classroom program designed to encourage respect and strengthen the connections among students from diverse communities while teaching them to celebrate the diversity and heritage unique to their own community.

BJ has a passion for excellence. She can confidently take a community project from start to finish with proficiency and ease. She instinctively creates a vision and then transforms it into a program of distinction. Then when each of her projects is complete, she humbly gives away the credit for it.

BJ's powerful passion motivates people to greatness by instilling a confidence in them that anything is possible. As a leader who has great character, BJ has an extraordinary commitment to serve that sets the standard for community workers to never settle for anything less than their best. It is not only a privilege for me to refer to BJ as an esteemed colleague, but it is also a profound honor for me to call her a friend.

Passion will draw an audience. People want to surround themselves with those driven by passion, because passionate people inject energy into an environment, and their enthusiasm consistently produces momentum. When passionate people speak, their words are laced with significance as both the tone and inflection of their voices naturally intensify. They continually demonstrate how deeply they believe in what they do. Their positive impact on communities takes place only because they are willing to devote their total being to fulfilling their purpose.

Another person who has this kind of energy and devotion to serving others is Mario Bucaro. To know Mario is to love him. His personality is magnetic, and his passionate drive for positive change is absolutely unstoppable. When I met Mario, he was the managing partner of Central Law, a law firm with offices in seven countries throughout Central America and the Caribbean.

Mario was also serving in the field of humanitarian relief and development as Operation Blessing's national director in Guatemala. I often wondered how Mario could meet all his professional obligations, take care of his family, and still have time to impact people's lives for positive change. The clear answer is that he has passion not only for people but also for strategizing new and effective ways to solve poverty's challenges.

When people talk to Mario, they feel as if they're the most important person in his world. If there are people who need his help, Mario is there for them. No matter what meetings are on his schedule, he will find time to spend with them. His commitment to serve others is inspirational.

When you see Mario in action, you know that his heart and soul are invested in delivering the message of hope and value to underserved populations. Mario is indeed a rarity, a man of incredible passion for serving his community. His noted accomplishments could fill an office wall, yet the title that I personally have given him—and one I think he has earned—is the People's Champion.

Passion is oxygen to a person's soul. It bridges the inward strength of a dedicated heart to the outward demonstration of devoted service. Passion pumps energy into the hearts of those committed to making a difference in their community, and it becomes intricately woven into their every act of kindness. Passion cannot be taught. It is instinctive.

Lynne is a friend of mine who lives and breathes to serve the needs of young people. She is devoted to community service. Lynne is a perfect example of a person who engraves her signature on the lives of others because of her unending supply of passion. I have had the pleasure of working with Lynne on several community projects as she has served children and youth living in untenable situations. It is her passion that led her to devote her life to serving others and not herself. Lynne, like every frontline soldier who is willing to sacrifice without hesitation in protecting the lives of others, knows the familiar sound of passion's call.

A Passionate Warrior Changing Lives

Lynne is a passionate warrior who gets into her car each day and drives directly into the world of the rough, tough, abused, and confused. Why? Because Lynne has a "you first, me second" passion for the forgotten, the unloved, the unlovely. Every day of her life Lynne is on a mission to make an impact in communities that city planners would just as soon delete from the map and that policemen would agree hold little hope for positive change.

The kids from these neighborhoods are considered at-risk. Their behavior is disruptive, and their tempers are explosive. Most of them experience a lifetime of tragedy by the time they reach junior high. They learn how to survive in their world by successfully building concrete barriers around their hearts. Lynne's passion burns so intensely for these youth that she has become a bulldozer for the walls surrounding their hearts. The fight in Lynne is relentless, and when it comes to her commitment to the well-being of these kids, her passion is unyielding.

Lynne has a small and fragile frame, but when she stands next to the kids she loves, her passion makes her look like a giant. For several years Lynne has fought a personal battle with a debilitating disease that puts her continually in and out of hospitals. One would think that in her condition Lynne would not have the strength to bulldoze walls. Where does Lynne's ability to fight come from?

She will be the first to tell you that it comes from her passion. You see, her passion does not have to be pumped into her as do the intravenous fluids she receives during her hospital stays. It will not run out the way the time does between her doses of pain medication. Passion has consumed Lynne's soul. She is on the front lines, reaching children living in communities the world says are not worth the effort. As long as she has breath, her passion will give her purpose.

Lynne is making a difference in the lives of "her" kids. She invests every ounce of her energy into creating opportunities for these kids to find a way out of their world. Exposing these young people to right choices opens their eyes to new possibilities, giving them a glimmer of hope for a promising future.

One time Lynne transformed an empty room in a neighborhood youth center into a reading library for some of her at-risk kids. It started when Scholastic Inc., a community-minded company that cares about making sure all children have an opportunity to read, donated to the youth center an assortment of storybooks at multiple grade levels. When Lynne saw the boxes of books, it nearly took her breath away as she simultaneously expressed her overwhelming appreciation for Scholastic's generosity. Her passion kicked into gear, and she immediately set out to create a place of refuge for her special children.

Lynne convinced one of her friends to paint a delightful mural on one of the walls depicting children reading books in the park on a sunny day. The other walls were painted with children reading books in a variety of different settings. Another friend of Lynne's built the needed bookshelves, and to complete the library, a local department store donated a couch and a couple of comfy chairs.

Lynne's transformed library was a sight to behold. One little girl told Lynne she had never been to a library—in fact, she didn't even know the meaning of the word *library*! With a warm smile Lynne put her hand into the little girl's, and the two of them began a special journey that opened this precious little one's eyes to a whole new world of learning and adventure.

Lynne's passion continues to spur on generations of kids whom she has rescued from a life of despair. Recently Lynne received a phone call from one of the girls she had helped years before. This young woman called Lynne to let her know that she was happily married and starting a family. She also wanted

Lynne to know that she was going to be working with children in one of the at-risk neighborhoods in her city so she could give back to others what Lynne had given her. When Lynne told me about the call and the new direction this young lady's life was taking, we shared tears of joy and thanksgiving. Lynne, the passionate warrior, had indeed conquered the impossible!

Living "You First, Me Second"

I hope Lynne's story has prompted you to think about how you can integrate passion into your life and embrace the "you first, me second" mind-set. Perhaps you've already started thinking about your own passion and how you personally can make a difference in the lives of others. Here are a few ideas to help you passionately get to the heart of social responsibility:

1. Start by making a list of activities that you truly enjoy. Examples might include watching or playing football, golfing, doing arts and crafts, singing, cooking, painting, repairing things around the house, fixing cars, or playing the guitar.

2. Prioritize your list, placing your favorite activity at the top. Your first-place choice should be something that you absolutely love doing, even when you are tired or have had a bad day. It should be an activity that you know will renew your energy and make you feel better. Here are a few more tips to determine what is your first choice:

- Engaging in this favorite activity is never drudgery to you.

- It is always relaxing and fun.

- You know a lot about this activity.

- You really enjoy talking with others about this favorite thing, because your knowledge about the topic seems to have no end!

- If you are still wondering what your first-choice activity might be, ask someone who spends a lot of time with you to give you his opinion. The answer might come quickly!

- Another way to identify your favorite activity is to look around your house—perhaps there are a number of books sitting on your shelf about your favorite pastime, or there is equipment in your closet that you have ordered to play your favorite sport. Maybe there are supplies tucked into a corner that you bring out when you want to engage in your activity, or perhaps there are tools in your garage that you tinker with when you are looking for a good stress releaser.

3. Once you have prioritized your list, take your top choice and consider different ways to integrate it with serving others, which will give it purpose. Below are some suggestions:

  - Let's say watching and/or playing football is the activity at the top of your list. To inject purpose into your passion for football, you could invite a couple neighborhood kids whose dads may not be around to come to your house and eat snacks with you and your family while you watch a game together on the television. I'm sure you would enjoy explaining the different plays the quarterback calls or offering substantive reasons you may not agree with certain calls the referee makes.

- As you spend time being the resident football "expert," you will find that you are having great fun and may even be a little disappointed when the game is over and your guests have to leave. However, your passion will have purpose because of the message of value the neighborhood kids will take home with them after spending an afternoon with you. I guarantee that your willingness to spend time with your new friends will create a memory the kids will cherish for a long time.

- If you have time, you could arrange for you and a couple of your friends to meet regularly with a small youth group to teach them football skills or to just go outside to do some free punting, passing, and kicking exercises. You could gather at a local park or even in your backyard. My guess is that within that group of young people there will be at least one person you're impacting merely by including them in a small slice of your life.

When passion becomes entwined in your "you first, me second" lifestyle, you will reflect genuine pleasure in investing your time in the lives of those you want to influence in a positive way. The key to extending your passion to others is to be sure that you already love that activity. When you stick with what is at the top of your list, it will never feel like extra work for you, nor will you become bored or tired of the activity. There are no words to describe the impact that spending time with people can have, especially those who may be experiencing pockets of emptiness.

Here are some additional suggestions for giving your passion purpose:

- If you enjoy the arts, teach a community class on music, art, or dance appreciation.

- If you are a natural mechanic, volunteer to repair or to change the oil in a single mom's automobile.

- If you love kids, offer to watch the children of a single dad or mom so he or she can take a break.

- If you are naturally handy around the house, see if there's an elderly person in the neighborhood who needs you to fix something that's broken.

- If you like to cook, volunteer to prepare and serve meals at a homeless shelter.

By giving of yourself to others by doing what you already love to do, passion creates significance that stretches far beyond the activity. Once you see that the time you're spending with others is making a difference, your passion will spur you on to want to do even more!

How and where do you find people to invest in? You may not have to look too far, as there are probably more needs than you can count right in your own neighborhood. Other places where you can get involved would be local churches, community centers, or nonprofits. The question is, are you willing to take your passion and invest it in others so that it can become a mechanism to transform lives?

Chapter 8

Being Honorable

Then the other administrators and high officers began searching for some fault in the way Daniel was handling government affairs, but they couldn't find anything to criticize or condemn. He was faithful, always responsible, and completely trustworthy.

Daniel 6:4

ONORABLE PEOPLE CAN be counted on to make sound and balanced decisions based on the fact that they give full consideration to the well-being of others before their own. Their actions are deliberate and consistent, which reinforces the credibility of their character. One of the greatest compliments a person can receive is to be defined as trustworthy by those who know him best.

Because honorable people live out the core value of uprightness as a lifestyle, their decisions will consistently be principle-driven. Their reputation of integrity will always precede them. They gain the respect of others because of their core values and the solid work ethic consistently demonstrated in their lives.

Through their own example, principled leaders will carry the responsibility of maintaining a lifestyle of honesty and integrity, and in doing so they will forge a path others want to follow. Honorable leaders have an innate ability to persist in a task with creativity and hard work, yet they also know how to communicate with compassion. These individuals want to achieve the best results without compromising or cutting corners. With honorable people their word is their bond.

When people are upright, who they are will be revealed through their character. Truth and integrity are the two principles of character that guide an honorable person's life. For these people walking out an honest lifestyle is a daily pursuit. They value being consistent in what they say and how they live. Have you ever been tempted to exaggerate a story, even just a tiny bit? Or do you find yourself fudging the truth just a little to help you get out of hot water?

These behaviors may seem minor in the big picture of life, but an honorable person will live out the truth even in areas that appear to be less important. The goal for the honorable person is to be grounded in the truth. People of integrity recognize that stretching the truth jeopardizes the integrity of their word and that truth stretched is no longer truth at all.

When you are honorable, the care you give to others also will be laced with the power of humility. In today's world the reoccurring message we hear is all about success, notoriety, and achievement. Because of this people tend to work all their lives to elevate their status or to attain a certain level of greatness. However, people with honorable character are not glory seekers; rather, they guard their hearts against pride. You will not hear honorable people refer to themselves as humble, nor will they boast about their own humility. Instead, humility will be tucked deep into their character, and they will clothe themselves with meekness as they quietly and effectively serve the people around them.

Today's world is in desperate need of principled people who can offer it stability and consistency. Those who are struggling with issues of hunger and dwindling supplies of food or who have lost their jobs or homes or who are slipping through the cracks of the educational process urgently need honorable people to rise up and serve their neighbors in the midst of desperate times. The dependable and consistent behavior of those who are upright will shine like a city set on a hill, and those who are in the midst of darkness will be drawn to their light.

The cries from those living in the grips of despair continue to be for those who care enough to intervene. The honorable person knows how to break down the protective walls surrounding the hearts of desperate people and to deliver the message of hope. Honorable people have a genuine compassion and a desire to avoid judging others, and those traits penetrate the lives of those who need it most. From this kind of care emerges one of the most treasured words in the English language: *trust.*

Trust does not just happen. It evolves out of someone's consistency. When a person exhibits integrity, he does things in a steady and dependable manner. When we reach out to people in need, the greatest testimony we can give them is the reliability of our actions toward them. People who are struggling through tough times are vulnerable and sometimes very defensive. The honorable person will demonstrate service to hurting people without depending on their receptivity or their behavior in the situation. His choice to stay the course and continue to serve with an attitude that gives everything and expects nothing in return will speak volumes to those who are in need.

The honorable person will be hesitant to make promises because of the detrimental effect a broken promise can have. Too many people have lived with the consequences of broken promises and have their guards up when they hear the words, "I promise." Instead, the principled person will let the testimony of his actions speak for itself. The consistency of such a person's presence and the reliability of their words are vital to building trust into relationships.

Honorable people make tremendous leaders because of their faithfulness to serve others without manipulation or the pursuit of self-gain. They have strength of mind to stand for what is right and can motivate others to follow them with confidence. They give genuine support and sincere advice to those they lead, and they know how to transfer their beliefs to the lives of others through their consistent example of dependability. Their strength of certainty gives them a natural ability to mentor those who are searching for someone to trust. Let me introduce you to Britni, the senior member of my staff who typifies a leader who follows her convictions with passionate intent.

Unwavering Credibility

It is rare to find a person with the confidence to grow a business, impact a community for change, and revolutionize lives through positive transformation, but Britni is a young woman whose character has produced this winning combination. Britni and I work together in the daily operations of product acquisition for global humanitarian relief programs.

Before Britni came to work at our organization, she had been employed by a small business owner to help him get his new business off the ground. When I first interviewed her, I asked why she wanted to leave the small business since it was such a success story. She said she wanted more. She wanted purpose in her life and had envisioned herself eventually being in a broader, more expansive role. Working for a global humanitarian relief organization would give her the opportunity to transform lives and impact at-risk communities all around the world.

In the workplace Britni manages the acquisition of thousands of truckloads of food and supplies that are distributed each year, free of charge, to those who have fallen on hard times. She oversees a staff that respects her leadership and her consistent and unwavering management style. Her dependability has given people the assurance that no matter what, Britni will not abandon ship and leave her team without its captain. Britni will absolutely not negotiate her core principles or compromise her standards of conduct. Britni is a confident young woman with true grit and a determination that is unstoppable. When she wants to ensure that the needs of others are being met, she is relentless until the delivery of care becomes a reality.

Britni is proficient in merging relationships with others and stays connected with her corporate contacts by communicating with them on a continual basis. As her corporate relationships grow, Britni looks for opportunities to transform them into partnerships for the purpose of community investment. Such is the case with her relationship with Coca-Cola, a community-minded company with an exemplary outreach to people around the globe.

Britni has been able to grow a relationship with her Coca-Cola contacts because of her integrity. Coca-Cola has given donations because they are certain that their refreshing beverages will be effectively and efficiently distributed nationwide to underserved communities. Britni's consistency in upholding the highest standard of product handling has won her the trust of her contacts at Coca-Cola. Britni knows how to create a perfect fit between corporate and nonprofit partnerships for the benefit of communities around the world. She is a young woman highly esteemed among those of us who have the privilege to be a part of her world. I am confident that her friends at Coca-Cola would agree that Britni is the "real thing" indeed.

Britni has a drive that is unstoppable when it comes to providing for people in need. She has a tender heart for children plus a committed resolve to see young girls on the brink of despair rescued from their prisons of hopelessness. She currently invests her personal time into the lives of girls and young women between the ages of eleven and eighteen. In a curriculum Britni and a friend of hers wrote, each lesson affirms the value of young ladies by focusing on ways for them to build their self-esteem. It guides these young girls and teens, some of them robbed of their innocence through circumstances beyond their control, to discover the beautiful person each of them is within.

The girls study individual character qualities that release true beauty from the soul as well as how to apply those qualities in everyday life. The ultimate goal Britni has for each of these special young lives is a changed heart, a transformed mind, and the successful application of life's truths, which promise to set them free. Once a year Britni hosts a special event for all the girls in her program. She calls this time her

Princess Weekend. Over the course of two days the girls are lavished with affirmation of their inward beauty, and as a result they can finally embrace the security of being loved, hope for a promising future, and an anticipation of great things to come.

Melanie was a special young lady who went through Britni's course. While she was in high school, she encountered many challenges that put her character to the test. She will be the first to tell you that the principles she learned through Britni's mentoring are what gave her the strength to fight through difficult times and come out a winner. Melanie is now in her third year of college and works as a summer intern assisting the leader of a local organization that serves victims of sex trafficking. Is Britni's investment into Melanie reaping benefits for others? Melanie will be the first to attest to the fact that indeed it is!

As a sincere and genuine leader Britni guides her students on this special journey of restoration and inspires them to believe in not only who they are but also in whom they can become. When she talks about her "princesses," her smile warms the room.

Britni lives and breathes for the purpose of serving others. Her heart pumps with passion for people, especially those who are in need. Whether a person is the president of a corporation or without a job, whether a person lives in a mansion or sleeps on the streets, whether a person is a scholar with multiple degrees or one with no education at all, Britni treats everyone the same.

Through her gentleness she is able to navigate a path straight to people's hearts, and in a matter of minutes she communicates to them her total acceptance. She meets people right where they are, and in no time at all they feel comfortable and safe enough to pour out their souls. If someone from any walk of life needs help, and if Britni knows about it, she will do everything possible to offer assistance by bringing relief to the person's wearied soul.

Those who demonstrate the kind of integrity that is fueled by purpose and devotion to God are destined to influence the lives of those they touch. With hearts that are dedicated to serving God and mankind, these people will instinctively intertwine devotion with gentleness as they journey through life. Their lives are a testimony to their faith, their dedication to serve, and their devotion to meeting the needs of people.

Let me introduce you to Stephanie, a young woman who is devoted to serving the God she so deeply loves. Her commitment and depth of character exemplify the "you first, me second" dedicated servant that she is—someone who is constantly giving of herself for the benefit of others and expecting absolutely nothing in return.

Persistent Integrity

Stephanie grew up in a family that was dedicated to serving God. Her dad, now retired from the US Navy, set an example for her through his faith and service as a dedicated chaplain. Stephanie is the most positive person I know, and her faith in God gives her a fresh perspective every day as she eagerly anticipates opportunities to serve.

Stephanie currently works with children and teens at a local Navy chapel. She also manages programs that reach out to the young men and women serving in our armed forces. She invests herself in their lives with a powerful dedication and an unwavering commitment. She organizes community get-togethers so that troops can relax and meet new friends. Her consistency of character allows even her newest military friends to feel at ease around her. The words she shares with the troops are as soothing as a fresh summer breeze, and her joy and laughter are contagious.

Because of her great respect for the men and women who serve our country, Stephanie wants to send a message to the soldiers she meets that their service is deeply appreciated and their lives are of great value in the sight of God. She demonstrates to each of the soldiers that her word is her bond, and the integrity of her life lays the groundwork for building relationships on trust.

Stephanie also has a special love for orphans, and her commitment to care for these parentless children extends to different countries around the world. Over a period of four years she worked with a children's home in Brazil, where she devoted her time to loving little ones. There was one special young man at the children's home, Alex, whom Stephanie met on her first trip there. This teenager's heart had become hardened because of the difficult circumstances he had experienced in his young life. Alex's father was unknown, and when Alex was very young, his mother struggled with alcohol addiction.

One night when Alex's mother was passed out, she accidentally rolled over on his baby brother and smothered the child to death. Not long after that his mom abandoned the remaining children, and Alex was sent to the children's home. With genuine concern for Alex Stephanie committed to show him love with the hope that he would realize that she truly cared. Alex was shy and withdrawn and suffered with a chronic ailment in his eyes. Stephanie accompanied Alex to the hospital multiple times. Alex continued to keep his defenses up in his relationship with Stephanie, but she was determined to love him, expecting nothing in return.

Stephanie visited Alex over the next few years and continued to stay in touch with him until there was a breakthrough in her relationship with him. Alex opened his heart to God and became a changed young man at the age of seventeen. He found a wonderful young lady who had been living at another children's home, and as the two of them planned to marry, Stephanie was able to help the young bride-to-be find her perfect wedding dress. Today both Alex and his wife are in full-time service at another children's home in Brazil. Because of Stephanie's authentic compassion for Alex, a true legacy of love will live on for generations to come.

Stephanie also dedicates many hours to prepare special packages of audio Bibles in a variety of languages. She sends them directly to orphanages so the children can listen to God's Word in their own languages. Stephanie's excitement cannot be contained when she sees her efforts create a full circle of care for orphaned children—not just physical care but also spiritual and emotional support as well.

Stephanie is committed to caring for people with the love of God that is rooted in her soul. Her devotion runs down to the very core of her being. Everyone who knows Stephanie agrees that she is one of a kind—a servant who truly exemplifies dedication to God and to the people she serves. How incredibly blessed this world is to have Stephanie, and how humbled I am to have the privilege of calling Stephanie my friend.

Living "You First, Me Second"

Each of us should want to impact lives for change and project to others an authentic "you first, me second" character. How can we make sure we are doing that? The trait of being genuine rests on one basic principle: being consistent with your words and dependable in your actions. In your service to others there are four principles to keep in mind as you work to build a more authentic character.

Love and accept people just the way they are.

When you work directly with people who need your help, create an environment in which they feel free to be themselves without fear of judgment. Be careful that you don't project intimidation or discomfort when you are in their presence. Remember that your reaction should not be dependent upon their behavior but should rather come from deep within your genuine character.

Be consistent.

As a health educator I always promoted eating well and staying away from fast food as much as possible. I told my students over and over that when making good choices became a regular part of their day, it would soon become second nature. I tried my best to be a good role model for them as well.

I remember going to a drive-through for lunch one time. I ordered a plain baked potato with the butter and sour cream on the side (so I could make my own decision on portion control) and an unsweetened iced tea. When I pulled up to the window, lo and behold, there was one of my students. When she saw me, she looked at my order and said, "Wow, Ms. E., I guess you really do eat the way you tell us to. I'm glad I didn't catch you trying to pull a fast one over on our class!" I have never forgotten that incident, and I use it to continually remind myself that people are watching our behavior whether we like it or not. Consistency will become your silent spokesperson.

Drop your expectations.

Do not arrive at your place of service thinking you will change people to become just like you or who you think they should be. Instead, put on your cloak of humility. Recognize that you are no better than the people you are serving, and if circumstances were different in your own life, it could be you in need of help. When you arrive without a set of expectations, then you will not leave disappointed.

Celebrate your differences.

Community service should be a time for you to interject words of encouragement, humorous stories, or just smiles of acceptance into people's lives. You can look at your time of service as two worlds temporarily coming together and two people possibly linking hearts. The celebration occurs when you realize that you've touched a heart and made a difference in someone's life. You will see that we are really all the same and that more often than not only circumstances divide our worlds. Being authentic allows you to love your neighbor without condition. It is truly the freedom we've all been created to enjoy.

Chapter 9

Being an Advocate

Yes, speak up for the poor and helpless,
and see that they get justice.
Proverbs 31:9

A N ADVOCATE IS a person who will take a lead role in speaking out in support of another person or cause. An advocate may be given opportunities to speak from a podium in front of a large audience, during a small breakout session at a conference or workshop, in the boardroom of a large company, into a reporter's microphone at a community event, or perhaps in the living room of a prospective donor to his or her organization. Or he may be given an opportunity to write a letter on behalf of individuals or an issue.

Wherever and whenever you are called upon to be an advocate, you need to be prepared to powerfully represent your cause. The best advocate is the informed advocate, which is why it is critical that you gather as much information as possible regarding the person or cause you are representing. The more aware you are of who or what you represent, the better advocate you will be. Your information should be delivered in a forthright and compelling manner. The better prepared you are, the greater your chance of getting noticed and being heard.

Teachers are great "you first, me second" advocates. They know what their students need, and when they are able to plead the case of a student in a difficult situation, they boldly take a stand. Below is a story about my oldest sister, Lynda, who was a stellar teacher of children with special needs.

An Advocate for Special-Needs Students

Lynda recently passed away after a two-year battle with cancer. As a professional she was a highly respected leader in her field of special education. Her area of expertise was teens with emotional needs. At many times throughout her career Lynda found herself serving as an advocate for her students.

When a teen in her charge struggled with inappropriate behavioral outbursts, instead of removing the student from the classroom or suspending him from school, Lynda would head to her principal's office to speak out on behalf of her student's potential rather than his disruptive behavior. She often negotiated for alternative rehabilitation plans to help her students learn from their mistakes rather than having them isolated or removed from campus.

At the beginning of each school year, as one of the experts in her field, Lynda would be asked to speak to fellow teachers about going beyond classroom responsibilities and embracing becoming advocates for special-needs children. Lynda once told me about a young man she tutored after school to prepare him for graduation from high school and acceptance into college.

She spent hours combing through this student's records to find noteworthy, positive things he could include on his college application. She guided him carefully through the application process. Lynda also talked with this young man at length about what he needed to write for his entrance exam essay and then walked him through every step of the writing assignment. She also made several calls to college administration offices to ensure that this student's application would meet the criteria required for acceptance. Not once did she wane in her belief that this young man would overcome any challenges he had.

As his advocate, Lynda projected her confidence into this student, and sure enough, against all odds, his application was accepted. In Lynda's eyes the future for this young man was filled with endless possibilities. Even though Lynda is no longer on this earth, her advocacy lives on in the hearts and minds of her students. She continually fought uphill battles on behalf of special-needs youth, and the impact of her strides will be felt for generations to come.

If you are a baby boomer or have parents in retirement, your advocacy role may include managing care for yourself or your aging parents. In today's complicated health care system, with its bureaucratic red tape, you may be serving as an advocate for your loved ones in doctor's offices, hospitals, nursing homes, insurance companies, banks, law offices—and the list goes on. The importance of being an advocate for a loved one is vital, especially one in crisis. You must become a voice for them.

The key to providing optimum care for your family member or loved one is becoming aware of laws, learning which legal documents need to be prepared and signed, and finding out if there are any living trusts or wills that need to be updated. You should know about alternative care solutions that you may need and possible temporary options such as nursing homes and rehabilitative hospitals that would be available in the short-term. You should also be aware of the documents already included in your loved one's health care portfolio, as well as the anticipated duration of health insurance coverage and the details of any long-term health care policies. Most importantly you should be given power of attorney so that you will have a clear understanding of how long your loved one's finances will sustain him.

This information only scratches the surface of all you will need to help a family member navigate the health care system. My niece and nephew were incredible advocates for my sister when her health declined, but they would be quick to say that the experience was overwhelming and at times the paperwork was suffocating. The end result of their advocacy was the fulfillment of exactly what my sister had requested: her orderly and peaceful departure from this earth as she was surrounded by her children, siblings, members of her extended family, and treasured friends.

In much the same way my niece and nephew were advocates for my sister, this world also needs advocates who will rise up on behalf of local community needs or for international humanitarian crises. If you work for a charity or a community-based business, you should be prepared to represent your organization to the public sector. You not only need to be knowledgeable about the mission behind your charity work, but you also should be actively promoting it! In your role as an advocate, you should be able to explain the purpose of your organization along with the kind of work that distinguishes it from other nonprofits.

Your communication to others must include a confident justification for the work you do. When people ask me about my job responsibilities, I tell them that I share the needs of those who are suffering with company representatives who have the tangible or financial means to help meet those needs. My job is to connect the resources to the need. When I am asked why I do this kind of work, I tell people that it is because I am called to be an advocate who will plead the cause of those in need and who have no voice. I have embraced the responsibility to speak on behalf of others in order to acquire resources that will restore lives and bring about change. Whether it is the delivery of hope to an individual or the total transformation of an impoverished community, as an advocate I am committed to maximize every opportunity I can to speak out on behalf of others.

Advocacy at Ten
Thousand Feet in the Air

I once had the pleasure of sitting next to a gentleman I'll call John while on a short late-night flight from Charlotte, North Carolina, to Norfolk, Virginia. I had been on another flight earlier that evening that had attempted to land in Norfolk during a storm called a nor'easter. The weather had been too severe to land, so the plane had been rerouted to Charlotte. About three hours later I was finally able to get the last seat available on the final flight to Norfolk.

The seat just so happened to be in first class, which became quite an opportunity. I can count on one hand the number of times I've sat in first class on a plane! It was about midnight, and as I sat down I smiled and introduced myself to John, the very weary passenger sitting next to me. He asked me what I did for a living, and even though it was late, I enthusiastically turned into an advocate.

Within just a few minutes I was able to articulate my responsibilities in a concise yet compelling way. When I finished, it was clear that I had gotten John's attention. He asked me more about the organization where I worked and about my role. I was able to share with him the smorgasbord of everything we do by using one hand. I put my thumb up and said, "Hunger relief," then up went my index finger when I said, "Disaster relief." With my third finger I added, "Medical aid," my fourth response was, "Safe water solutions," and with my fifth finger extended, I said, "Orphan and vulnerable-children care." All the good work we do around the world was wrapped-up in a short and to-the-point presentation.

As an advocate you may have only a short period of time to deliver the information about what you do or the cause you represent, so preparation is vital. In this particular instance John was somewhat of a captive audience (on a plane on which we had to keep our seat belts buckled the entire flight!). But by my being prepared, John gained a deeper understanding of the needs of the people Operation Blessing serves. I also was able to tell him how a donation of the paper his company manufactured could help meet some of those needs.

As our conversation continued, I learned that John worked at a large paper company, and as a result of our dialogue he asked if we could use paper donations in any of our programs. "Of course," I replied, and I began to tell John about the different community projects we sponsored that could definitely use his paper. There were lots of after-school programs we sponsored across the country plus hundreds of community partners that could benefit from a donation of paper. Many of those partners could actually redirect their limited funds to other areas if they didn't have to worry about purchasing paper. I told John that indeed, a donation of paper would be a huge encouragement to our network of community partners.

It turned out that in one of John's recent business transactions, there had been a printing error on the packaging of multiple reams of paper, and John's buyer had refused to accept the order. The paper needed to be moved out of his warehouse, and when I told him we had a fleet of trucks that could come pick up whatever paper he had available, John smiled, shook my hand, and told me that we had a deal. John's donation turned out to be a tremendous blessing for our partners in the field. If I had not been prepared for my advocacy role, the man from the paper company sitting next to me may have just as well opted for a nap on his way to Norfolk rather than for listening to what I had to say.

Advocacy for Needs in Chicago

I had another advocacy opportunity when I visited Chicago for an appointment with a gentleman named Phil. Phil worked in the corporate offices of Subway Development Corporation of Chicagoland. When I arrived, he gave me time to share about my organization and the work we were doing in Chicago. Because I had prepared in advance, I was familiar with the areas in Chicago we had targeted to provide assistance, the location of our community agency partners, how many people we were currently helping, and the list of our most pressing needs.

At the end of my plea Phil was eager to help. As a result of our meeting, he offered to create a plan of action to help raise money for our needs in Chicago. In the plan Phil designated a day he called "Operation Blessing Day in Chicagoland" on which the proceeds above daily operating costs from designated Subway stores would be given to support our work in Chicago.

Phil put us in touch with Subway's local marketing and public relations firm so we could map out the details. From that office we were given guidance and offered several suggestions on how to inform our support network of the designated day. The firm also gave us ideas about how to motivate new customers to visit neighborhood Subways on that day. And we were given a timeline as to when we should complete different action points in order to ensure the best results.

Everybody worked hard to put together a day that would benefit the work Operation Blessing was doing in Chicago. The project was a great success, and Subway Development Corporation of Chicagoland was able to give us a large financial gift designated for our Chicago community efforts. Subway held a presentation in one of its stores, where we received an oversized check about four feet long and two feet wide. Camera crews and reporters conducted interviews. It was great to see how advocating for a need had come full circle and how speaking out for the needs of others strengthened a community's work.

An Advocate to Fight Hunger

There are times when people you know will become an advocate for you or your organization. This happened to me through a relationship I had with Kenny, who at the time was managing the Baltimore Ravens community relations department. When I initially shared the idea with Kenny about having a large-scale community food distribution event, he immediately became an advocate for our program.

His enthusiasm generated full support from the Ravens players, and as a result, the Ravens hosted the first of many events with us in the city of Baltimore. On the day of our first event a huge bus arrived to the site filled with enthusiastic Ravens players who quickly debarked and navigated their way to different workstations. Their dedication and energy was a sight to behold as they actively participated in sorting, bagging, stacking, and distributing thousands of bags of groceries to people hungry and in need.

Kenny's enthusiasm spurred the Ravens players to commit to making this an annual event. His advocacy for fighting hunger also resulted in M&T Bank committing to provide employee volunteers and a local grocery store chain to deliver a truckload of food to each event. Kenny's advocacy continued to expand the program, and it wasn't long before the Baltimore mayor's office and the city's employees had become an integral part of the event's planning and implementation process.

As an added feature, one year the mayor arrived at the site to personally greet local Baltimore residents with a handshake and a smile. Along with the mayor came a barrage of reporters, which helped us in our efforts to inform as many audiences as possible about the hunger issues in America.

In continuing his "you first, me second" advocacy, Kenny became our promoter to his contacts at UPS in Baltimore. As a result of Kenny's advocacy, many UPS employees became enthusiastic volunteers looking forward to the event each year. Because they had such rewarding experiences connecting to the people they served, the UPS employee-volunteers became advocates themselves. They shared their excitement about their community service with the UPS corporate headquarters, and their enthusiasm resulted in a large financial contribution from UPS to support our hunger-relief efforts in Baltimore.

When the right people are in an advocacy role, their endorsements will yield numerous benefits that keep multiplying as more people become informed. When you are asked to be an advocate for a need, your preparation and readiness will surely elicit a spontaneous and firm "Yes, by all means!" from you. Then you will ask the question, "Where and when do I get started?"

Living "You First, Me Second"

Are you ready to be an advocate? Did any of the examples above get you thinking about your own advocacy role within your sphere of influence? The wonderful thing about advocacy is that you can be an advocate for only one individual or for a whole world of people.

As an advocate your passion and drive to make a difference combined with thorough preparation will enable you to profoundly impact those who need you to be their voice. Below are a few advocacy opportunities for you to consider. You could speak out on behalf of:

- Military widows

- Wounded veterans

- Food pantries

- After-school programs
- Homeless shelters
- Life-skills and job-training programs
- Soup kitchens
- Clothes closets
- Battered women's shelters
- Unwed mothers
- Orphans
- Children with terminal diseases

Being a "you first, me second" advocate to represent people who have needs is a privilege, and yet it is also a heavy responsibility, because it requires preparation, time, availability, confidence in public speaking, and a relentless drive to speak out on behalf of someone else. Being an advocate provides you with an opportunity to testify to the needs of people and then help others identify ways they can make a difference. Those who have been on the receiving end of an advocate's work would be the first ones to say that the value of your advocacy is priceless!

Chapter 10

Being Inspirational

That is why we never give up. Though our bodies are dying, our spirits are being renewed every day.
2 Corinthians 4:16

NSPIRATION COMES IN many forms. For some of us it comes through reading a good book or viewing a magnificent work of art. For others it is wrapped up in the beauty of nature—the splendor of a sunrise splashing beautiful hues across the early morning sky or the majesty of a waterfall crashing with such power that it takes our breath away.

Sometimes our inspiration can come through people we admire. When I think of evangelist Billy Graham, I am inspired. One day I wrote the words below about the power Billy Graham projects not because of his prestige or popularity but through his humility and quiet, unwavering faith.

> Billy Graham leads with the prowess of a lion, yet he serves with the gentleness of a lamb. He hosts

evenings of fine dining for honored guests and then willingly gives away his place at the head of the table. He addresses crowds with inspiring messages, and his speeches conclude with thunderous applause, yet he will stop to personally thank the person who swept the stage in preparation for his arrival.

Inspiration, no matter what form it takes, has a way of refreshing us and renewing our strength. Many of us have people in our lives we can call upon when we are going through tough times. In the midst of our own difficulties we are drawn to those who have the wisdom and insight to keep us focused as we navigate stressful situations. The words of these principle-driven, wise counselors are inspirational, and they renew our strength.

These people—pillars of integrity—keep us balanced throughout our tumultuous times. When a boxer is on the ropes, the referee knows just when to blow the whistle and call time-out. In a similar way inspiring people know just when to offer wisdom and give a fresh perspective that will get us off the ropes of life and back in the ring to face another round.

Inspiring Commitment

When I think about people who inspire, two individuals immediately come to mind. Their names are Bob and Mary Fanning. Mary passed away a few years ago after a valiant battle with Alzheimer's disease. Before she was diagnosed, Mary invested her time in me, and she gave me very wise counsel about some critical issues I was facing in my life. I was definitely in an arena of conflicts, taking lots of punches and unexpected jabs. I was inspired by Mary's wisdom and refreshed by witnessing firsthand how she applied the principles that guided her life. She had modeled a life of integrity, so I knew the counsel she gave me could be trusted. I heeded her advice, and life got better. For me, that is.

Mary's life took a turn toward an illness that most people dread the thought of. When she was in the early stages of Alzheimer's disease, Bob, her faithful husband of over fifty years, retired from his job in order to take care of his lovely bride. For a few years he was able to care for Mary at home, but as the disease progressed, Mary needed a level of care that he could no longer provide. Bob found a new home for Mary in a lovely care facility and brought in many of her most precious belongings, including pictures of the two of them together with their children and other loved ones.

Bob's devotion to Mary is what I personally find so inspirational. From the early days of her disease to her final months of struggle Bob was by Mary's side. Every day without fail he visited Mary so they could be together in their "second home." What is truly inspirational to me is that for a very long time, Mary did not recognize Bob at all. He and others in the family would talk about memories they had made together, but Mary remained unresponsive. I can only imagine the heartbreak that Bob and their children must have experienced during these very dark days.

Bob also served as an inspiration to the staff at the care facility where Mary stayed. Every day they saw him faithfully arrive for his visit with Mary. He took the time to get to know staff members on all the shifts, and he offered encouragement to them, even in the midst of his own struggles. Bob became an advocate for the Alzheimer's Association regarding research, treatment, and care of the disease, and for years he has participated in special fund-raising opportunities to support the association's local efforts.

Today Bob is in his eighties. I recently bumped into him at a community event, and he was kind enough to spend time listening to everything I had going on. I updated him on some of my professional endeavors, and later that evening I received an e-mail from him with some additional thoughts about our conversation. I was touched by the fact that he had listened so intently to me and then had taken the time to offer wise suggestions. Bob made me feel valued, and that in and of itself was soothing to my soul.

I am truly inspired by Bob, who has lived through the progression of a disease that in time took his beloved wife from him. I personally think that Bob should be a spokesperson for the Alzheimer's Association, as his wisdom, integrity, and principle-driven life could be used to inject hope and strength into the hearts and minds of people living through the same dark situation he and Mary endured with such grace.

Bob's steady presence beside his wife as she valiantly battled Alzheimer's was an inspiration to many.

People who work on behalf of those in their community can also be an inspiration. Too often the deeds of these faithful workers go unnoticed, but when we are given the privilege of seeing firsthand their commitment and dedication, it can take our breath away. This happened to me recently when I visited North Carolina. Deep in the foothills of Appalachia, where the need is so huge it can leave you wondering how to even begin to offer help, I met a very perceptive pastor named Lee. The enormity of the need didn't paralyze Lee. He reached out to his neighbors by helping to revive and refresh their spirits.*

Providing a Meal— and Sharing Kindness

Pastor Lee has a soft spot in his heart for children, and when he learned that so many little ones in his county were going hungry, he began a weekly feeding program that is now touching families who had been convinced that no one cared. Every week there is a message posted on the marquee outside his church inviting families to come and receive a free hot meal. I asked Pastor Lee how many people usually attend, and he told me between fifty and one hundred fifty, depending on whether families had enough gas in their cars to make the trip.

The Appalachian foothills have many winding roads that lead to homes tucked away deep within the mountainous terrain. Making the trip to Pastor Lee's is not easy for the people of his county, but knowing that a hot meal will be served is enough motivation for individuals to do what they can to make it there. On the night that I was there, more than one hundred people came to the gathering to get some nourishment—and to receive the kind of care and understanding they needed.

As each family arrived, they were greeted at the door with handshakes and hugs, and then they were personally escorted to a table decorated with a lovely tablecloth and candles. Once seated, a volunteer came to take people's food and drink orders. In a very short time the meals were brought to the table and served to each of the family members. I noticed that the menu

---

* Pamela Erickson, "Falling Through the Cracks," Operation Blessing newsletter, December 2011. Printed with permission

items that night came from a table in the front of the room lined with Crock-Pots, casserole dishes, and nine-by-thirteen-inch pans filled with items specially prepared by faithful volunteers.

As the guests dined, some of the local teen talent provided soft music. Following the meal, families were invited to visit the small food pantry in the next room to fill empty bags with groceries that they knew their family would eat. Pastor Lee's perception of these people's struggles was evident in his tender care of each honored guest. He was inspiring to watch throughout the evening, but two specific moments captured my heart.

The first was after each family finished their meal and got up from the table. I noticed that a volunteer rushed to put down a fresh, clean tablecloth before the next group arrived. I asked one woman why fresh cloths were put down when surely the others had not been terribly soiled after just one family's meal. She responded by telling me that the fresh linens were just one small way to demonstrate to their guests their incredible value to their friends, family, church, and, most of all, to God. To me the dinner was a royal feast at a table set for a king.

The second observation that touched my heart was when I watched the parents visit the small food pantry. Each family received an empty grocery bag for each of their children. I watched the parents shop for free, looking for the items they knew their children would like. I thought about what it must be like to be a hungry child. For them, eating food items they liked would make coping in their world a little bit easier.

I also thought about how difficult things must be for parents who intensely struggle to feed their children. Pastor Lee cares deeply for the people of his county, because he understands that asking for help is not easy. He is always looking for ways to help people in the situations they face so they will not lose hope. He is indeed a gentle giant living in the Appalachian foothills who is playing a huge part in caring for his neighbors. His joy is not only in the giving of provisions but also in the building of trust among those he so faithfully serves. To me that is inspirational.

I am sure there is at least one person you know who puts others' needs before his own. It does not have to be on a large scale, with thousands of lives being reached—it is just as inspirational to see one person extending himself for the benefit of another.

Once while visiting Chicago, Illinois, I had an opportunity to visit Kraft Foods, a company committed to community investment. The purpose of my visit was to share about the work we were doing in Chicago and to explore ways our organizations could partner with Kraft on projects targeting some of the city's most critical areas of need. Because I had a limited amount of time, I felt inspired to share with the woman I was meeting with a story about a friend of mine named Jim. He is a man from the Chicago area who has focused his life's work on helping people, both on and off the clock. His demonstration of care was indeed an inspiration to me, and all those who know what he does when the rest of the world is sleeping will agree that Jim is indeed one of a kind.

"You First, Me Second" Inspiration

Jim is now a retired police detective, but he worked for over twenty years on the west side of Chicago. You can't get a beat much tougher than that. I witnessed firsthand, however, a passionate side of Jim that surfaced during his off-duty hours. On a very cold Chicago winter day I arrived in the city to visit Jim, one of our faithful community partners. Shortly after I checked into my hotel room, I received a call from him. He strongly encouraged me to catch an afternoon nap, because what he had planned that evening would keep us up all night.

Twice a month like clockwork Jim ventured into the world of the forgotten. At eleven o'clock on this particular night, he and I journeyed together along with a small group of faithful volunteers into a dark and cold existence. Jim's passion was clearly the fire that lit the path for our travels that night. Inside the nooks and crannies of the concrete jungle of freeways and overpasses Jim introduced us to the drifters of this world, people without direction, whose lives were without purpose. At the very top of one embankment was a small flat surface lying parallel to the overpass that at least half a dozen men called home. None of them seemed to be bothered by the noise of cars rocketing above their makeshift refuge.

When Jim came into view, the men called him by name as if he were one of their own. Their eyes radiated a warm glow that could have melted the Chicago icicles hanging from their unyielding concrete dwelling. Their frozen lips cracked hearty smiles, and their voices echoed laughter even through the whistle of the brutal winter wind. We helped Jim give everyone we met that night a bag of groceries, hygiene items, and blankets to keep them warm. Along with a hug or a pat on the back Jim gave each of the people we met a verbal affirmation that he sincerely cared. You could tell by the response of each man that he knew Jim's words came from his heart.

Jim and I sat and talked with one elderly man who told us of his earlier life. He shared the circumstances of how he had fallen on tough times and how his livelihood had plummeted.

With tears in his eyes he told us that he was unable to get out of the hole he had dug for himself. He opened up his wallet and showed us a picture of his grandchildren and said that one day he hoped to see them again. It was when I saw the pictures that I realized that all these men were real people with real lives and real needs. They were people just like Jim and me.

It was about four in the morning when Jim dropped me off at my hotel. As he walked me to my room, I realized that as a detective, Jim was committed to protecting lives and keeping people safe. As a man devoted to his city, Jim had a passion for mankind that went far beyond his job. His love for people extended in limitless directions to individuals from all walks of life. Every person we visited that night, no matter what his story, had a place in Jim's heart. Jim may not make the headlines of Chicago's newspapers, but he has most assuredly gained fame by having etched his love on the hearts of those he considers a precious part of his life, the royalty of his world.

When I finished telling Jim's story to my contact at Kraft, I knew her heart had been touched. Why had I been so compelled to share about the homeless men sheltered beneath the freeway overpass? Because Jim had inspired me, and I knew that the group of homeless men I met that night was only a small representation of a larger need. If it were possible for my telling Jim's story to connect the need to those who had resources to help, then my mission would be fulfilled.

There is nothing like making a memory and then sharing that memory with people who can make a difference. Without the inspiration of this off-duty detective, my presentation would have included only statistics and cold, hard facts. As it turned out, we received a financial contribution from Kraft Foods that was designated to help the homeless in Chicago.

Today Kraft Foods, now two companies, Kraft Foods Group and Mondelēz International, are both committed to community investment.

I had become inspired by watching Jim in action. His "you first, me second" demonstration of care to the homeless was incredible to see. Because I walked side by side with him, I'd had a genuine, hands-on experience of caring for some of the city's most vulnerable residents. Going out with Jim that night in the brutal winter weather was my choice. No one forced me to participate. I had actually looked forward to going, because I love people and I respect Jim for what he does for others in his off-duty time. His devotion to making Chicago a better place extended out in multiple directions, and I was privileged to see his commitment lived out.

Seeing Jim's loyalty to this special group of men was life changing for me. If they were to consider how late we were out and the places we visited, many people would shake their heads and tell me I was crazy to even think about going out with Jim. But Jim had been serving the homeless of Chicago for years, and I was confident to trust him and to follow his lead. It was a long way up the freeway embankment that night, and the only way to climb the concrete wall was to walk up sideways, taking small baby steps. I had some misgivings about halfway up, but I was determined to meet those men and to find out more about their lives. I will never forget the feeling of accomplishment I experienced when we finally reached the top of the embankment and connected with that special group of men and helped to meet their needs.

When your stories about serving others include your own firsthand experiences, those stories will have an even greater impact on the listener. Because you were there and saw the need—you smelled the need, touched the need, listened to the need—when you left, the need became a part of you. Being able to share this kind of depth of insight through your personal accounts can truly be inspirational to others.

Here is inspiration's secret: If you allow yourself to become immersed in the lives of those who are being crushed by circumstances often beyond their control, you will be inspired by their stories. Their stories then become yours to tell again and again, and each time you share them, you will be inspiring someone new.

Living "You First, Me Second"

Would you like to be inspired? If so, hearing the stories of those who are on the front lines of community and charity work will get you started. If by chance you work at a company that is community-minded and interested in its social responsibility, consider arranging a meeting with other staff members and implementing a week of inspiration:

- For each of the five days during your week of inspiration invite one or more representatives from a locally based charity to come to your workplace and share about their community work and the ongoing needs they face.

- Ask your guests to be prepared to share personal stories. If possible see if they can bring one community resident whose life has been changed because of the help received from their charity. Be sure your guests share details about the changed person's life both before and after their charity intervened.

- See if you can have one staff member take pictures and another write a summary of each presentation.

- Perhaps you can include the speaker summaries from your week of inspiration in your company's internal newsletter.

- Encouragement is another way to inspire people, so you may want to consider doing a few things to make the guests from your featured charities feel appreciated for the work they do in your community. Here are a couple of thoughts:

  - Feature their stories on your company website with a link to the charities' websites.

  - Send each of them a written thank-you note from one of the company's executive leaders.

If you want to be personally inspired, the best thing you can do is make an appointment to visit with the executive director of your charity of choice. This is where you invest your time to learn more about the people the charity serves as well as the circumstances surrounding the individuals' struggles. The leaders of these organizations will be able to tell people's stories with great insight and intense passion. Even if your meeting is relatively short, you will be inspired if you listen carefully to what the leader says. You may even want to get involved personally. Ask probing questions about the individuals who are served and how the charity is making an impact in their lives.

During your visit, ask if you may have a tour of the facility. If there are classes or other activities in session, ask if you can take a peek at the instruction going on while you're there. Look at the faces of the children who might be learning to read or about healthy eating, watch the eagerness of the teens preparing to take their GEDs, or connect with the adults being taught how to better manage their finances. These are real people with real struggles, just like you and me.

Chapter 11

Being Relationship Driven

Love each other with genuine affection, and
take delight in honoring each other.
Romans 12:10

THOSE WHO ARE relationship driven have a passion for people. When they meet someone for the first time, they know how to ask the right questions to discover common interests. They are comfortable in just about any setting. From sitting on a couch watching TV with a friend to waiting in long lines with perfect strangers at an amusement park, the relationship-driven person will feel at home. If there is someone in her midst, the relationship-driven person wants to engage in some kind of conversation.

Relationship-driven people are naturally friendly and outgoing, and they have a knack for easily relating to others. Because they understand that every relationship is unique, they can tailor their conversations to gel with diverse personalities. A relationship-driven individual is a people person. He is the one who greets you with a "good morning" when you arrive at work and wishes you a "good night" when you leave in the evening.

When relationship-driven people ask, "How are you?", they really want to know, because they care. If you let them know that you're not feeling well or are struggling with an issue, they will come back later to find out if things have gotten better. They convey sincerity in their every word, because authenticity is imbedded deep within their character.

Those who are relationship-driven are astute and able to demonstrate excellence in their exchanges with others. They remember where a conversation left off and can reignite the same dialogue at a later time. If they say they will get back to you, you can expect them to do so. They keep their word and are as dependable as the dawning of a new day.

Relationship-driven people are essential for every business, especially those committed to connecting with their community. These keen individuals are experts in jump-starting conversations. Even when making or receiving cold calls, to them no one is a stranger. The following conversation could have taken place at any customer service–based business on any day of the week. What made this encounter extraordinary was the perceptive person who happened to answer the phone.

Customer Service Extraordinaire!

One morning Kathy, who is part of our corporate donor-relations team, received a phone call from a woman I'll call Ms. Brown. Ms. Brown was looking for some assistance. She had been working for a long time on updating her financial portfolio, and she needed to have a few questions answered. She also was planning to contact her bank regarding her financial decisions, and she urgently needed to speak to someone who could immediately give her the answers she was seeking.

Kathy was reassuring in her response, and in her warm, calming way, she let Ms. Brown know that she would be sure to connect her directly to the right person. First, Kathy gave Ms. Brown the name and extension of the person in our organization who could answer her questions. Knowing the urgency of Ms. Brown's request, instead of transferring her call and risking the possibility of Ms. Brown getting a voice-mail, Kathy kindly asked Ms. Brown if she could put her on hold. She assured Ms. Brown that she would not be more than a minute and would check to make sure the staff member with the answers would be at his desk. Ms. Brown agreed to hold, and Kathy scurried down the hallway.

Seeing that the contact was in, Kathy gave him a quick overview of Ms. Brown's situation and let him know that she would promptly be transferring the woman's call. Kathy rushed back to her desk. She thanked Ms. Brown for waiting patiently and let her know that she would be transferring her call immediately. Kathy also told Ms. Brown that she was very thankful she could help her get the answers she needed. Ms. Brown responded with a sigh of relief and thanked Kathy for being so kind and helpful.

Instead of immediately pressing the transfer button and risking losing Ms. Brown's call, Kathy let her know that she would stay on the phone through the transfer process to make sure the call connected. When Kathy heard Ms. Brown and the other staff member begin to dialogue, she completed the transfer by hanging up her phone.

Kathy is a relationship-driven, intuitive person. The combination of those two qualities guarantees excellent customer service, because a person who has those traits understands the needs of others and makes those needs a top priority. When Kathy first answered the call, she immediately detected that Ms. Brown was in a hurry and wanted answers to her questions right away. Kathy masterfully navigated the conversation so she could find out exactly what Ms. Brown was looking for. By responding in a warm and reassuring way, Kathy was able to give Ms. Brown confidence that her questions were important and that she would make sure that they were answered.

The skill of moving through conversations to establish rapport is an art that perceptive, relationship-driven people attest comes as naturally to them as breathing. What they bring to a customer-focused company or organization is invaluable not only to the business but also to the people it serves.

When people build business relationships that are anchored in a commitment to invest in communities and individuals in need, these relationships will be tied together with strength and purpose. Great relationships are birthed when people work together for the benefit of others. Whether your responsibility is to provide resources (financial or product), help develop a program, or manage the implementation of a project, strong and powerful relationships will emerge between you and the people you partner with because your focus is on the common goal of meeting needs.

Successful relationship mergers result when a company donates a product to a charity to benefit others, and that charity in turn delivers the company's resources directly to the individuals in need. Recently I took a very unique group on a tour of one of our distribution centers. This was a group of students, most of whom were under the age of ten. As we toured the facility, I was able not only to show the children the products we are able to give to people in need but also to reflect on the relationships that made those donations happen.

A Relationship Tour

When the children first arrived for the tour, their eyes grew as big as saucers because of the massive size of the warehouse. They were amazed as they saw all the stacks of pallets loaded with various products. They loved watching the forklifts picking up and unloading supplies. One of their favorite moments was when the forklift backed up and made loud beeps. I explained that those sounds were warning signals for people to watch out and to stand well out of the way.

We followed one of the forklifts to the back of the warehouse, where trailers were being loaded with products to be delivered to people in desperate need of the supplies. The children saw another trailer being backed up to a dock door. I shared that the trailer would soon be unloaded by another forklift and the product taken to a section of the warehouse where all of it would be resorted and then put on another truck for delivery somewhere in America. One of the students asked me where all the products came from. It was then that the former teacher in me jumped at the chance to explain to the children that what they were seeing was more than just "stuff"—that actually behind every donation was a significant relationship merger.

We first stopped at some pallets of drinks that had been donated by Dr Pepper Snapple Group (DPSG). I shared that these were much more than just bottles of drinks; they were gifts that had been given to help people. I told them that the most important thing about the drinks was who had given them to us. It was then that I shared a story about how I met my friend Mil.

I was first introduced to Mil when I made a call to DPSG inquiring about drinks that might be available for donation. Mil listened intently to a few stories I shared about people I'd met who were struggling to feed their families and said she would do everything she could to find out if DPSG had available drinks for us.

I told the children that in my conversation with Mil, I learned that she lived in New York City and, just like me, she loved to help take care of people who were struggling through tough times. Mil did find some drinks that were available for us, and that is how a very special friendship began.

I also shared with the children that the donated drinks were helping us take care of people all across the country and how very generous DPSG had been to provide the beverages for so many people in need. One little girl responded by saying that she was going to tell her mom to make sure to buy DPSG drinks the next time she was at the store. I'm sure her words would have put a big smile on Mil's face.

As we continued on the tour, we soon arrived at the pallets of books from Scholastic, Inc. This is where I told the students about Karen and how hard she works to support community-based reading programs all over the country through her donations of her company's brand-new books. I shared how Scholastic, Inc. had helped to provide a community center not too far from our warehouse with lots of books for kids of all ages. The community center leader was able to transform an empty room into a cozy reading room where children could come to enjoy the adventures of reading.

I told the students that Karen also knew how children loved to play games and to work with arts and crafts. She made a special effort to donate several bins of Scholastic, Inc.'s Klutz books for us to deliver to children who might not get new books, games, or crafts very often. I pulled a couple of samples out of a bin next to me and showed the kids a book on how to play jacks and another one about how to make beaded necklaces. The students really liked the Klutz books. I told them that when I had been a teacher, I had used the instructions in a Klutz book to teach my students how to juggle with scarves.

Several students asked where they could buy the books, and when I told them, they were resolved to convince their moms and dads to take them shopping that very day! I wish Karen could have seen the excitement coming from the children. She would have been so energized by their enthusiasm. Karen and Scholastic, Inc. certainly know how to generate the love of reading and learning into the hearts of children everywhere.

Our next stop brought us to huge pallets of stacked banana boxes filled with every kind of product you can imagine. The children viewed lots of different items in the boxes, including cans of fruit and vegetables, granola bars, cereals, and candy. There were other items also, such as detergent, shampoo, lotions, and so much more. I said, "All these boxes were given to us because of my friend Scott." I told the students that Scott is a grandpa and that his grandchildren say he is the best grandpa ever!

As we started to move on, one little girl noticed a package of diapers in one of the boxes and said, "Oh look, my baby brother wears diapers like these." I replied that because of the diaper donations, we can help moms who sometimes run out of diapers when they have no money to buy more. I shared how one young mother, with her little baby girl in her arms, came to a distribution in hopes of receiving a donation of food. She didn't know that in addition to the food, diapers were also available.

When she saw the diapers, the young mother burst into tears. The children wondered why she had started crying, and I was able to tell them that for the two days prior to the distribution, the young mom had been using paper towels as diaper substitutes for her little girl. I think this vivid picture of the reality of people's need was most likely being seared into the children's minds that day. The children and I walked to the next section of product in silence.

Next we came to a stack of smaller boxes that looked like they were ready to be put in the mail. They were not on pallets but separated. I told the children that we had just received the boxes from my friend Ben who works in the community relations department of the Kansas City Royals. The team had donated some baseballs and T-shirts for children who lived in an orphanage in Somaliland, a country on the continent of Africa. "Whoa!" the children gasped. "Africa is really far away."

I asked them if they knew what an orphanage was. Some raised their hands or nodded, and some remained quiet. I asked one of the little girls who had nodded if she would like to share the meaning of the word *orphanage*. Her explanation was that it is a place where children who don't have a mother or father or anyone else to take care of them live. She added that she thought an orphanage must be a very lonely place.

I agreed and then told them that my friend Ben has a real heart for helping children and other people who are in need. I told the children that because he cared more about others than himself, he would do anything for anybody. One of the children asked if Ben had his own collection of autographs from the Royal players. I replied that I was sure he had been to many autographing sessions, but that knowing Ben, I was confident that any autographs he may have received were probably for someone else.

Right next to the baseballs and T-shirts were special items such as baby powder, baby lotion, diaper rash ointment, and other items the orphanage desperately needed. The children asked if Ben had given those items as well, and I said, "No, these are from my special friend Janice, who works at a company called Chattem, Inc. located in Chattanooga, Tennessee." I told them that when Janice found out about all the children in the orphanage, she cried. She then told me that she was going to do everything she possibly could to find a product that would be perfect for the babies. I knew in my heart that Janice's love for children would result in her making sure that the children in Somaliland would have some Chattem, Inc. products to help meet their needs. One little boy commented, "I think my mom would like Janice." I chuckled and said, "Yes indeed, I'm sure she would."

At the final turn in the warehouse we came to a fenced-in area where medicines destined for countries all over the world were being stored. This is where I told the students about my friend Kipp, who had worked with me for more than ten years. One of the children responded, "Wow, that's even older than me!" I told them that Kipp is the father of two girls and is a big Georgia Bulldogs fan. He loves to go to his older daughter's dance recitals and also enjoys watching his youngest daughter, who is a cheerleader. He really loves to surprise his family by doing nice things for them. One time he put together all the plans to surprise his wife with a party for her fortieth birthday. He took care of every detail without his wife knowing anything about it. The party was a big success, and everyone was amazed that Kipp had been able to keep a secret that big.

I told the children that when Kipp isn't with his family, he is some place in this world checking on medicine programs and making sure the programs are helping people in those communities get better health care. One of the children asked, "Like where?" I answered, "Well, he's traveled to countries in Africa, Latin America, Europe, and South America." By the time I talked about each of the countries where Kipp had worked, I felt like the children had benefited from a great lesson in geography! The students also realized that the job of making sure medicines are delivered to people in different countries takes a very special person with a giant-sized heart. I thought about Kipp, and I couldn't have agreed with them more.

After the children left that day, I took a few minutes to walk back down some of those aisles of palletized product. I reflected on the relationships behind the pallets and realized how blessed I was to have such meaningful friendships that had been created for the purpose of caring for the needs of others. The children left that day with the assurance that people really do care about one another, and I'm sure they went home with their own stories to tell. I wish I could have been in each of their homes to hear what they shared. I'm convinced it would have brought great delight to this teacher's heart!

Each relationship is unique indeed. Like our fingerprints, every person is different, and the qualities each one brings to a relationship are specialized and distinctive. If relationships are healthy, vibrant, and growing, they will contain two important elements. The first is time. Because relationships evolve over time, the quantity of time people spend together will determine the depth of the relational bond. The individuals may not spend a lot of time together in the beginning of a relationship-building process, but as a friendship matures, the investment of time will naturally increase.

The second element of a healthy relationship is sacrifice. Some may think of sacrifice as requiring a level of pain, but relational people put the needs of others before their own without much thought. When it comes to relationship building, sacrifice is when we surrender ourselves on behalf of someone else. It is much like when you make plans to go to dinner with a friend. You may want to go to a certain restaurant, but your friend prefers another. When you willingly agree to go to the restaurant of your friend's choosing, you are surrendering yourself for someone else. Now that wasn't so painful, was it? Of course, there are more complex illustrations involving deeper sacrifices, but the point is, thriving relationships require both parties to give and receive.

Whatever we invest in a relationship will determine how that relationship matures. If we are introduced to someone, have a short conversation with him, and then part ways, the person we met would be simply an acquaintance. On the other hand, if we nurture a relationship, it will develop into a friendship. As we invest more time into the friendship, it will deepen and become a companionship. This is when a relationship becomes comfortable enough for both parties to relax and be themselves. With more nurturing, companionship develops into a level of commitment through which hearts and lives become intertwined.

The highest level of intimacy we can experience is in our relationship with God. The Bible tells us in Psalm 139 that God knows everything about us. He knows when we sit, when we stand, what we think, what and how we do things, and what we are going to say before we say it. God has us enclosed within His protective care, and His hand is always upon us. He knows where we go, and He promises never to leave us.

We can have confidence that He securely holds onto our hand. We have His assurance that when we are in darkness and cannot see, He can see us. As our Creator He knit us together, and before we were even born, He knew every fiber of our being. When you think about the intimate level of His involvement in creating every fiber of our being and the time He put into shaping us into exactly who we are, the most precious thing we can do is give back to Him our time and build an intimate relationship with Him that will last forever.

Living "You First, Me Second"

Do you want to become more relational? Below are some tips to help you begin. You can actually incorporate a few simple ideas into your life that will strengthen your ability to build relationships.

Cultivating friendships

Do you want to create new friendships that will last?

- First, make a list of the most significant relationships that you currently have. Don't be concerned with the length of your list, as quantity is not important.

- Next to each name on your list, explain why that person is significant to you.

- Decide on a mode of communication you will use to contact each person, and write that method next to the individual's name. Then contact each of them and let them know that they are significant to you and why. Make a call, stop by for a visit, send an e-mail, or mail a handwritten note. Please forgo any texting, tweeting, or other forms of instant communication.

- If there is someone on your list with whom you'd like to spend some time, put a specific activity idea next to his name (i.e., watch a movie, have dinner, go out for coffee, etc.).

The purpose of this particular exercise is to take you from just thinking about someone to actually investing your time into nurturing that relationship. Remember that it takes both time and sacrifice to develop any relationship. The final step you can take in this exercise is to post your list in a place where you will be sure to see it every day. As you glance at the names of the special people on your list, stop and say a prayer of thanks that each of them is in your life.

Growing work relationships

For the relationships you have at work, here is an easy exercise to build healthy relationships among coworkers:

- First, see if you can get a calendar to hang on a wall or to display on your desk. Try to find

out the birthday of each person at your workplace, or at least of those who are part of your
department or team.

- Next, on the date of their birthday, write each
person's name on your calendar. If you think
you'll have trouble remembering to glance at
the calendar, ask someone in your office to
remind you each month to check your calendar for noted birthdays.

- Finally, make sure you approach each birthday
person on his special day, say, "Happy birthday!",
and start a conversation about what he might
be doing to celebrate the day.

People usually like to talk about their birthdays and about
any plans they might have to celebrate. If you discover that no
one is doing anything in particular to celebrate, do something
to celebrate your friend. If it's appropriate, you could suggest
taking him to lunch or dinner after work. At the least you
can circulate a card and give a small gift. The most important
thing is to take the time to let those in your workplace know
you care.

Enabling healthy partnership relationships

When working with others on community projects, communication is crucial to ensure that each person knows what
the others are doing. Follow these guidelines to make certain that healthy relationships continue throughout your
partnerships:

- Take time to meet with your team members face-to-face around a table.

- Visit each other's workplace to meet all the team members involved.

- Keep track of your progress through every step of the project by discussing the issues and action steps as they arise.

- Arrange occasional conference calls to which all participants (even those in less senior positions) can dial in so they feel like an integral part of the planning process.

- After the completion of the project call a meeting to discuss results. Make sure to value everyone's input.

- Keep communication open even after the project is finished.

When everyone is investing in the project, the relationships that will emerge are sure to be strong and lasting. Remember that the secrets to collaborative project partnerships include investing your time, putting the needs of others before your own, and keeping everyone involved.

Growing deeper in God

Having a desire to develop a deeper relationship with God is the first step on that journey. When you want your faith to grow, talk to God, and He will surely provide you with many opportunities to bring about that growth. Your part in the relationship will be to keep your desire for intimacy with Him vibrant, continue to talk with God and share the secrets of your heart with Him, become a good listener, start reading passages of Scripture that will reinforce your desires (start by reading Psalm 139), and have conversations with people you know who also are seeking to grow in their relationship with God. Then watch your relationship with Him unfold into something more intimate and beautiful than you ever could have imagined.

Chapter 12

Being a Change Agent

At last the wall was completed to half its height around the entire city, for the people had worked with enthusiasm.
Nehemiah 4:6

S OME PEOPLE DON'T like change. They will tell you that they prefer to follow a routine and maintain the status quo. They are more comfortable with staying under the safety net of predictability than with taking risks.

And then there are people who live for change. They think outside the box and love to problem solve. They look for solutions to make things function better, or they seek ways to make working systems run even more efficiently. Change agents see ways to improve projects, products, and procedures, whether they need a minor tweak or a major overhaul. If something can be improved, these individuals will be the first to offer a plan of action, a timeline, and a list of the incredible results that will occur because of the positive changes.

Change agents intuitively make things better. When they see a problem, their first inclination is to develop strategy to address it. Then they set incremental goals, if necessary, to implement a plan that moves the situation toward a positive resolution. They can break down challenges into manageable components and then address each aspect with great determination. Change agents are talented observers who see details that others frequently overlook. They tend to have an unending reservoir of creative energy and innovative thoughts when others have run out of suggestions, and change agents tend to offer just the right solution.

Change agents don't fret, because they know that worry consumes valuable, productive time. They purposefully turn from distractions, and they refocus their thoughts on what is rewarding and most beneficial. At the same time they guard against overload by wisely planning ahead and arranging their activities with precision. Their days are structured but not rigid. After all, change agents are always open to making adjustments. They most certainly allot time for unexpected interruptions and meet each one with gleeful anticipation of the benefit that will come from the temporary distraction.

Change agents are often hired to turn around a project or organization in decline, or to raise the bar of excellence. This person might be the principal hired to improve a struggling school, the coach brought on staff to improve a flagging team's record, the new pastor assigned to redirect the mission emphasis of a church, or the disaster-relief team mobilized to help rebuild a storm-ravaged community.

Change agents make great consultants for those needing help navigating personal challenges because they are such natural problem solvers and have the ability to organize a plan of action that yields a positive outcome. My friend Steve is a change agent who has great business sense and a strong mathematical aptitude. He has counseled many people through financially challenging situations and guided them to successfully break free from overwhelming debt.

He is a no-nonsense kind of guy who will gladly lay out an action plan—but he'll be the first to tell you that it will work only if you do your part. He will provide the guidance but will be frank in saying that financial restoration requires living within your means. That is not the message people under a mountain of debt often want to hear, but when it comes to turning a financial nightmare into debt-free living, Steve is the change agent you want on your side.

Companies hire change agents to analyze their processes and provide strategies that will improve them. These same qualities can be employed by those wanting to serve their communities. When businesses focus their efforts specifically on social responsibility or community investment projects, they want to ensure several results: that excellence will guide the operation, that they will have a positive community impact, and that they will gain a reputation as good corporate citizens.

In addition to making a difference in people's lives, a business wants to be known as a company that cares. With all this in mind someone who is a community-relations change agent would analyze what a company already has in place and then orchestrate changes that will enhance its effectiveness.

My friend B. J. Corriveau is one of the best change agents I know. She is currently the vice president of radio operations at the National Association of Broadcasters, but BJ and I worked together when she was the vice president of community and charitable programs at the Washington Redskins Charitable Foundation. BJ took on the responsibility of managing the annual Redskins' Harvest Feast. The event had been working well for years, but BJ was determined to take an already excellent program and transform it into an extraordinary one.

For many years the Redskins had distributed food every November at their stadium, FedExField. The invited guests would receive free bags of groceries that were packed by volunteers and then handed to them by some of their favorite Redskins players. Between two hundred fifty and three hundred corporate volunteers would work tirelessly to sort and fill grocery bags with a variety of special holiday products.

Within four hours these dedicated community servants would assemble over ten thousand bags of food for more than thirty-five hundred recipients. It was always an incredible sight to watch and a great example of community investment. However, when BJ the change agent examined the overall program, she saw opportunities to improve and enhance the benefits for the food recipients as well as for the community surrounding FedExField.

In the times we had together, I watched BJ take this quality community program and transform it into an amazing example of excellence by raising its operation to the next level. She accomplished this by committing her time, energy, and creative talent. BJ started the process of change by examining each component of the program, analyzing the efficiency of all operational aspects, and then developing a plan of action. This resulted in an event that has evolved into a well-oiled machine from start to finish.

BJ implemented her changes systematically to make sure each improvement yielded the desired outcome. She took ownership of the program with the goal of producing an event that would represent her distinct signature, which is to make things a cut above.

Taking a Project to the Next Level

When BJ was given the responsibility for managing the annual Redskins' Harvest Feast event, she began by thoroughly studying every detail of the program. She examined the volunteer activities, corporate partner involvement, logistics, community outreach, and the care being provided to the people who would be receiving the food.

In her review BJ noticed that there was no mechanism in place to prescreen the grocery recipients and no clear assurance that the event was serving those truly in need. The mission of the program was to help the underserved in the county where FedExField is located, but there was no guarantee that those coming to the event even lived in Prince George's County. Another variable involved the number of people who waited in line for the food. Even though a substantial amount of product was delivered to the event, there still was no guarantee that those who waited patiently in line would receive groceries.

Following her review, BJ came up with a great solution to these issues. She forged a successful relationship with the Prince George's County Social Services office, and together BJ and the Social Services staff implemented a plan that would guarantee help for the families who needed it most. By asking people to first connect with the Social Services office, those who wanted assistance would be screened to ensure they met the qualifications to receive food. A system was then put in place to guarantee that all who attended the event would receive the food they needed for the holiday. For BJ the partnership with Prince George's County Social Services not only made the event more operationally sound, but also more importantly it allowed the Redskins to more effectively serve those in need.

In her continuing pursuit of excellence, BJ also arranged to have a press conference at FedExField prior to the event each year. Some of the individuals she secured to speak at this press conference included the owner of the Washington Redskins, as well as other senior Redskins staff, corporate leaders, and nonprofit representatives. Through these press conferences each guest was able to tell people about what their businesses were doing in the area of social responsibility.

One of the most touching moments during these press conferences was always when members of the community would tell about their personal struggles and share what it means to them to have food for their families. During difficult times, receiving a turkey and holiday trimmings can help not only feed families in need but also give them hope. As people shared their stories, they shed tears, and for those listening, a sense of urgency seemed to arise that motivated them to meet similar needs in their own communities. Still today the press conference BJ initiated remains an effective way for area business leaders to communicate their intent to not only make a difference but also to show how much they value each individual receiving the food.

Another strategy BJ implemented was to have the players wear their jerseys to the event. This helped fans easily recognize their favorite players. It also provided photo opportunities that corporate volunteers could use to highlight their day of service and that nonprofit partners could include in their communications to food donors.

BJ's creative changes to the existing Harvest Feast event has made the Redskins program the standard for other NFL teams that host similar activities. The Redskins have emerged as the premiere example of an organization that is committed to providing its fan base with extraordinary community service with a high standard of excellence. This is what BJ the change agent is all about—developing new strategies to maximize efficiency, all while prioritizing the well-being of those she serves. BJ is most assuredly a "you first, me second" change agent who is committed to using her gifts and skills not to advance her own career but to serve others.

Living "You First, Me Second"

You don't have to manage a large staff or be the CEO of a major company to bring about the kind of change that will benefit others. All you need is the boldness to step forward and extend a hand to help improve your community.

As a change agent you will naturally want to turn a negative situation into a positive one or make something function better. The first step to becoming a change agent in your sphere of influence is to identify the need that is best suited to your gifts and talents. I promise, if you seek you will find, and before long you will be plugged in and bringing about positive change!

A change agent innately has the motivation of heart and the readiness of spirit to make adjustments in projects or programs so they will bring even greater benefit to communities. And they are willing to invest their time and talents, because "you first, me second" change agents find satisfaction in knowing that their efforts will help change someone's world.

The following ideas may help you to start thinking about ways you can become an effective agent for change:

- Perhaps you are a painter, and every day you drive by a community center that is in desperate need of a fresh new look. Instead of wondering when someone is going to get around to taking care of the problem, why don't you be the one to make the first move?

- Maybe you love to garden, and you notice that one of the houses you pass on your way to work has a front yard that you consider an eyesore. Instead of shaking your head in disbelief, why not put together a team of fellow gardeners and volunteer to give the yard an "extreme makeover"?

- As a talented seamstress you notice that the drapes in the school auditorium are discolored and tattered. Do you wonder if your talents are needed, or do you think you can't make a difference? Of course your skills are needed, and the difference you can make is to help create a place that teachers and students can be proud to call their own.

Change agents are innately prepared to make things better. They thrive on doing things that will improve the lives of others. Remember, the best way for positive change to occur is first to be aware of a need and then to have enough boldness to be the one to make the first step toward improving things. My question to all the change agents out in this world is, what are you waiting for?

Chapter 13

Being a Team Player

He makes the whole body fit together perfectly. As each part does its own special work, it helps the other parts grow, so that the whole body is healthy and growing and full of love.
Ephesians 4:16

TEAM IS AN integrated unit with a defined purpose. The main goal of a sports team, for example, is to win games; a sales team aims to close successful deals; the objective of a fund-raising team is to increase cash flow. Teams come together to accomplish numerous kinds of objectives, but the one objective every team must have in order to fulfill its purpose is unity. Team players—people who willingly work in cooperation with one another—are a must for a group that wants to bring about community impact.

A team can be comprised of two or more members, each contributing a distinctive personality and gifting. But even when it has many members, a team is most effective in doing extraordinary things when its members operate with a unified spirit. Team players are creative, people-focused vision catchers and skilled communicators. With so many different personalities and talents, how can unity be built into a team? The key to building team unity is for each member to show respect for the other members and for their contributions to the team's overall purpose.

An effective way to build unity within a team is for the members to spend time discovering the strengths, talents, and gifts that each of the others contributes to the team's strategic goals and objectives. The job of team leaders is to fully invest their time, energy, and creativity in order to strengthen the confidence of their teams.

I once had the privilege of leading a team through such a discovery process. Each team member, including myself, took a personal assessment to identify our greatest strengths. The results of the test would give us insight into the strongest skills we had to contribute to the overall effectiveness of the team.

To create a casual setting that would be more conducive to personal sharing, we gathered at a local coffee house to share what each of us had learned, and we verbally reaffirmed the strengths we had seen demonstrated in one another. I guided a discussion of how as a team we could use each of our areas of gifting to become a more dynamic, goal-oriented team. We talked about how each member's contribution to the team would be a valuable asset to achieving those goals.

This approach was successful in building team spirit, and at the same time it became an exercise in vision casting. The ultimate goal of a team leader is to guide each player to believe in the possibilities everyone can accomplish together. As each person embraces the confidence to forge ahead with great expectation, the dream of what could be will become his own.

Respect is a team essential, because it produces harmony and ultimately develops trust among the players. When you have unity that is based on respect, the team will go from measuring success by its performance to ultimately measuring success by its integrity.

If you look into the character of a genuine team player, you will see the sacrificial "you first, me second" mind-set at its best. Some may think of sacrifice as forfeiting or forgoing something, but in the "you first, me second" approach sacrifice is the actual surrendering of self for the sake of the team and, more often, for the well-being of others. It is the epitome of a selfless spirit. When a team is formed for the purpose of helping others, you will see unity, respect, and sacrifice mixed together to ultimately produce a group of very driven individuals.

A Night to Remember

Here is an account of a number of team players who rallied together to give several underprivileged young women a real sense of their true beauty and value. The story began with a donation of beautiful formal dresses to a nonprofit organization. Shortly after the formals arrived, I talked with a woman I'll call Elaine, who told me that she had heard about some teenage girls who for various reasons were not able to attend their senior proms.

A few of the girls came from broken homes, some from community-based programs for at-risk teenagers, and others from households in which there was a critical shortage of money to pay bills let alone provide for extravagant expenses. Elaine made a call to a woman named Carol, who worked at the nonprofit organization that had received the donation of prom dresses. Her plea for help came at the perfect time, because Carol had personally pressed out the wrinkles of each dress in the hopes that they could make a young girl's dream come true.

Carol was elated to tell Elaine that she had the dresses. Then she asked Elaine to find out what else the girls needed so she could help ensure that each girl had a night to remember. Once Carol received the list of items, she started networking around the community, and with every phone call she made she became more excited. In a very short time Carol and Elaine accomplished a great deal: one charity partner donated a brand-new elegant pair of shoes for each girl, and another organization donated several fine accessories.

Stylists from local salons willingly gave their time and resources to style the girls' hair and to apply their makeup. A special room was set aside for the excited teens to have privacy in choosing the perfect gown for their event and for all the last-minute primping before their dates arrived to pick them up.

A group of fine young men arrived to escort their princesses to a special dinner and dance. The donations for their evening included a limousine to transport the handsome couples to their destination. The team comprised of charity organizations, business leaders, and individuals from the community, each having different skills and personalities, had come together for the purpose of blessing these precious young lives. For the young people who received the outpouring of this kindness and sacrificial giving, it would indeed be a night to remember—forever!

When a team takes on a project that can affect the lives of people in distress, the action plan must include clear assignments and each person's designated responsibilities. Each team player is held accountable not only to the task but also to one another. By working together for the duration of the project, these team players will be able to develop a balanced workload and a focused momentum.

It is when team players depend on one another that they gain the strength to persevere through any project challenge. As a team gels, its members become inspired to support one another even through unexpected obstacles and seemingly insurmountable setbacks.

Our team at Operation Blessing encountered a variety of challenges when we gathered together to tackle the issue of transporting relief supplies to Haiti following the devastating earthquake that occurred on January 12, 2010. Here is our story.

"You First, Me Second" Team Approach

Shortly after the catastrophic earthquake struck Haiti, our team feverishly started putting together plans to help provide immediate relief to those impacted by the disaster. Our international relief team was dispatched at once to make assessments and to report the most pressing needs of the Haitian people back to headquarters.

One of the most critical needs in Haiti was water. The procurement team quickly immersed themselves in networking with their contacts for potential donations. It was not long before Dr Pepper Snapple Group (DPSG) had offered to donate bottled water. The first part of the response was now in place, but because there were so many challenges surrounding transportation and shipping capabilities in and to Haiti, we immediately called a team meeting to assess the situation and develop a strategic plan of action that could be implemented in as short a time as possible.

Steve, our vice president of operations and logistics; Doug, our director of transportation; David, our director of international shipping; and Larry, our director of warehousing, started unfolding the plan step by step. As all of us navigated what seemed to be insurmountable problems hindering our relief efforts in Haiti. Yet by bringing their expertise to the table, each team player began helping to solve the logistical logjam one issue at a time.

In the meeting we decided that a multifaceted approach would help us deliver the critically needed water to the Haitian people. Because runways at the airport in Port-au-Prince had been severely damaged in the quake, air shipment was not a viable option. Our next choice was to send the supplies by sea container, but the Haitian port had also sustained damage, and at that time there were no ships going in or out. The situation left our team with only one other option.

Because we already had a solid relationship with US Navy personnel stationed at the base in Norfolk, Virginia, Steve called his contact there to find out if there was a way we could work together. We learned that there was potential to have US Navy ships stage relief supplies a short distance offshore from Port-au-Prince and then to transport the product to land utilizing smaller boats. It sounded like a great plan, but collaboration between our staff and the US Navy would be a critical component to ensure that all the details and plans would meet everyone's approval.

Steve was invited to attend a strategy meeting at the naval base in Florida to further discuss the operations of the relief efforts. During his meeting at Jaxport Naval Terminal in Jacksonville, Florida, Steve learned that a US Navy ship preparing to depart for Haiti in just a few days had space for our water among its relief cargo. Steve called me from Florida with the proposed plan, and I immediately got in touch with my contact at DPSG to let her know that the US Navy would provide space on their ship to get the large donation of Snapple water to Haiti.

The water donation just so happened to be stored in a warehouse close to the Navy base in Jacksonville. Under time constraints Doug dispatched our fleet of fifty-three-foot tractor-trailers to Jacksonville. Upon our arrival at the warehouse we pulled the trucks up to the dock doors, where the warehouse crew started loading the trailers. As each one was filled, our drivers transported the water to the US Navy base. Once permission was given at the base's main gate, our drivers were credentialed and cleared to deliver the truckloads of water to the US Navy ship that was being loaded with other critically needed relief supplies for Haiti.

Over the next two days multiple truckloads of water were transported from the warehouse to the base. Through the joint efforts of our transportation and operations team, the team from the warehouse in Jacksonville, and the US Navy personnel loading the ship, in record time the water was on the ship and bound for Haiti. It was indeed a tapestry of moving parts being woven together with unity, respect, and a "you first, me second" attitude to accomplish what initially had seemed to be an impossible challenge.

But the story does not end there. After the ship's arrival in Port-au-Prince, the US Navy personnel unloaded the bottled water and the other relief supplies and transported them to the dock area. Our rented trucks were there to help transport the water to an available warehousing facility in Port-au-Prince.

From that facility the water was transported to the areas in which the quake had caused the greatest destruction. In the meantime Doug managed to catch a Mission Aviation Fellowship flight to Haiti and accompany one of the rented trucks as it delivered water and other relief supplies to an orphanage. There the children had been sharing bottles of water. Having four daughters of his own, Doug's heart was deeply moved when he arrived at the orphanage and was greeted by the cries of the elated children followed by grateful hugs for the water.

This mission had all the key elements of successful collaboration. If any part of the logistical plan had been removed, the plan would have lost its effectiveness. Because the team players held each other accountable for their assigned responsibilities and because of their integrity and commitment, not only were hurting people given sustenance, but also, perhaps, a glimmer of hope was restored.

Living "You First, Me Second"

Do you want to be a team player? Here are a few ideas to get you started:

- Contact a friend and suggest that the two of you start walking together. Choose a time that is best suited for both of you and schedule it. Commit to begin walking at a pace that is comfortable for you both. If you are able to talk without losing your breath, you'll be in a good place to start. Together you can accomplish the goal of becoming more fit.

- Ask a couple of coworkers if they'd like to get together every other week at lunchtime to have some casual conversation. Pick a conference room or an available office space, bring a bag lunch, and plan on being there for the sole purpose of building camaraderie. The benefits of the fellowship are incredible, and you'll probably find that in no time you are not only looking forward to those lunch hours but you'll also want to increase those meetings to once a week!

- If you are active and enjoy recreational sports, join a bowling league. These leagues offer great opportunities for team building, and a real plus is that you have the guarantee of being able to participate. There's always a spirit of competitiveness, but at the same time bowling is not as intimidating as other sports are in your effort to consistently be at the top of your game. The environment is also casual, and being around fun-loving friends can be a great stress reliever.

- If your church provides off-campus small groups or life groups, as they're often called, consider getting involved. You'll want to find out some basic information ahead of time such as the starting time, the meeting location, whether or not there is childcare, etc. Some churches have affinity groups for military families; empty nesters; those who are single, divorced, or widowed. Other groups target specific topics of the Bible or studies that have been put out by favorite authors. In any case, new members are always welcome, and the group may be exactly what you've been looking for!

• Whatever your interest might be, if you want to be a team player, finding a group should be your priority. Then as you begin to gel into a group or team, you'll find that building healthy relationships will be a big part of your success. Let others see the real you. Sometimes groups can be intimidating, but the more time you spend in your group, the more freedom you will feel to be yourself. As that occurs, your freedom of expression and sense of team belonging will be strengthened.

• Be committed to attending your group's meetings or gatherings. If you are haphazard in your attendance, you will send the message that the group is not a priority for you. I know there may be times when you cannot make get-togethers, but most of the time you should be consistent in your participation. This will let others know you are reliable.

- Follow through on any responsibilities you commit to handle. Your commitments could range from agreeing to search the Internet for additional information on a topic that came up in discussion to bringing snacks to the next gathering to saying you'll check up on someone who missed the last meeting. If you say you are going to do something but show a consistent pattern of dropping the ball, people will begin to realize that they cannot depend on you. They will then begin to ask others to take on the task assigned to you. Eventually you will pay relationship consequences.

Building successful relationships requires openness, commitment, and integrity. You must embrace these qualities in order to build trust between you and the rest of your team. Once your team or group is healthy, vibrant, and relationship driven, you are ready to add the "you first, me second" component. This can be accomplished by each team member embracing a purpose for your getting together that includes ways to help others. Think back to the four suggestions I made at the beginning of this chapter's action point. For each of those ideas I've added an additional thought for you to consider:

- For the two of you who are walking together, start a fund to which each of you contributes one dollar for every mile you walk. Then check with the head of one of the Little Leagues and see if you can purchase the athletic shoes that one of the children needs or perhaps even buy a child's uniform (depending on how many miles you walk!). In doing this, you will add a "you first, me second" purpose to your walks.

• For the group that is getting together for fellowship over brown bag lunches, you'll find that over time common interests will surface in your conversations. Let's say your group talks about how kids today face so many more challenges than you all did at the same age. Why not invite a guest speaker who works with teens on a regular basis to join one of your lunchtime gatherings to talk about the crises facing so many young people? Your guest speaker will make your team aware of the cold, hard facts of the obstacles facing youth today. As you become informed, your team members can then look for ways to help young people address one of the issues you've learned about. Then as a group you can impact your world!

• As you move through the bowling season, how about suggesting that your team get together on a Saturday morning to bowl with a group of preteens or teens. This would be a great way to get in extra practice between league nights and to give team members opportunities for one-on-one mentoring with kids—kids who may enjoy bowling but who are actually longing for time and attention. If you need help finding young teens, check with local charities or organizations that provide after-school care or community programs for kids.

- If you are in a life group at your church, designate a new charity each month for your group members to research online. Then when you meet together, make it a point to talk about the charity during your fellowship times. This way you will become aware of the needs of people not only in your circle of friends but also around the world. As that awareness grows, your "you first, me second" character will stir you into action!

Digging deeper

- Write your name on a blank sheet of paper.

- Under your name list all the strengths, abilities, or talents that you personally can bring to a team.

- Next, write down the name of another person on your team, and under his name, list the strengths, abilities, or talents you think he could bring to the team.

- Add at least four or five more names to your list, and write down those individuals' strengths also.

- Now examine the strengths you listed, and ask yourself the following questions:

  - Do any of the team members you listed have the same strengths as you?

  - Perhaps your top strength is organization, and one of the other players also has that strength. You know that you could do a great job heading up the organization. Would you be OK if the other player was assigned that responsibility? Or would you feel that you are better equipped for that task and assigning the other team member was unfair?

Let me leave you with this final thought. When you are willing to give away what you think you deserve, you are ready to be a team player!

Chapter 14

Being Generous

Whatever you give is acceptable if you give it eagerly. And give according to what you have, not what you don't have.
2 Corinthians 8:12

I BELIEVE THAT WE are all created to be givers. It is natural to want to give when we see a need, whether it is through our time, our skills and abilities, or our finances. Following the Asian tsunami in 2004, the number of people who gave financial support was phenomenal. The response would be equaled only by the worldwide reaction to Hurricane Katrina in 2005 and then the outpouring of aid that continues to flow into Haiti since the devastating earthquake in 2010.

We were made to give, and not only in response to disasters. Each of us has been created to help when we see a need. Some people commit their support to causes such as hunger relief or cancer research; others give financially to colleges and universities; some volunteer in international relief efforts while others participate in programs for orphans and vulnerable children.

Although all of us have been created to give, some people have a particular affinity for generosity. Charitable people are innately kind and compassionate, and when there is a need, they are the first to want to do something. They will act upon their desires in multiple ways, with one goal in mind: to make a difference!

Generous people give for the purpose of restoring and renewing hope in others. Those with philanthropic hearts are moved to action as they become aware of crisis situations and desperate needs. When people have the gift of giving, they often look for ways to scale down their own lifestyles and curtail nonessential spending in order to free up resources to give away.

People who love to give financially are usually good money managers. They know how to live within their means and to manage their spending, because they ultimately know that the more they have to give, the more people will benefit and the greater their impact will be. Givers are prepared to share on the spur of the moment. They create a plan of action for giving ahead of time that allows them the freedom to give without feeling shackled.

There are countless opportunities to offer assistance, and people who are generous will come out in droves when volunteers are needed. When the need is made known, natural givers with available time will be first in line to sign up to help. The principle of "you first, me second" is lived out to the fullest measure in those with a generous heart and a willing spirit. Generosity is at the heart of social responsibility.

Generous people tend to be spontaneous. When they can give surprise gifts, it excites them deep down in their souls, especially when their acts of kindness far exceed what the recipient may have expected. Below is an example of one such surprise.

Happy Birthday!

I am sure that each of us has experienced at least one special birthday in our lives. I have had several very nice celebrations, but there was one particular birthday on which I was surprised with a gift that truly took my breath away. It was one of those milestone birthdays that most women don't want to admit they are having. In honor of the occasion, somehow Cathy, my assistant at the time, managed to put together a scrapbook filled with photos, personal letters, and notes written by my family members and dear friends.

In order to pull this off without my knowledge, she had started working on it months before my birthday. I found out later that she had collaborated with my mom and with one of my sons to gather addresses and pictures of all the special people who would be featured in the album. Cathy mailed out decorative sheets of paper for each person to compose a handwritten note to me. She was able to contact many of my friends, some from as far back as twenty or thirty years. Cathy requested that people send as many pictures as possible of themselves and me together.

Using her administrative and creative gifts, Cathy compiled all the personal letters and pictures into a beautifully decorated album, with each page dedicated to a special person in my life. When she gave me the album as a birthday surprise, I started flipping through the pages, and my heart welled up with emotion. I read through some of the letters and looked at the pictures that family and friends had included on their pages, and I was honestly at a loss for words. Cathy's gift to me clearly required an investment of many hours of her personal time. Knowing that she had devoted that much of her time to create my surprise made me realize that her generosity was truly a gift. To this day that scrapbook remains a treasure to me.

Cathy's gift is a perfect illustration of "you first, me second" generosity. The giving of someone's time and talents was for the sole benefit of someone else. What Cathy created for me is irreplaceable. Now that my mom, dad, and sister are deceased, their letters and photos have even more meaning for me. Recently I found myself flipping through the pages again, because I wanted that warm, comfortable feeling that only being around loved ones can bring. Every moment of time Cathy spent creating that masterpiece has produced hours of enjoyment and reminiscing for me. Her gift will definitely keep on giving.

It is always a distinct honor to work with people who exhibit generosity as a lifestyle. My friend Justin is a perfect example of that. He is a giver whose heart is in tune with the needs of people who struggle with hunger in America. Here is a little more insight into this man I call my friend.

A "You First, Me Second" Giver

Justin, who ran the former Griffin-Holder onion company, is an extremely charitable man. When times were lean, Justin would tell me that his company had to tighten its belt and that they would have fewer surplus onions to donate. But when they had no extra product available, Justin would do the unexpected.

He would start making phone calls and networking with other onion growers to see if anyone else had onions available for donation. Because of his intervention, many times we still were able to pick up enough onions to fill our fifty-three-foot tractor-trailer.

Justin's generosity extended well beyond what one would anticipate from a donating company. It was apparent to me that other growers in the area had a genuine respect for Justin and for the way Griffin-Holder conducted its business. The company had a reputation for integrity and excellent customer service. Even as a company executive Justin embraced the "you first, me second" mind-set.

There were occasions on which Justin would spend time talking with me on the phone. He was always interested in learning more about the current needs of our organization and how charities operated. It was during those conversations that I realized Justin had a true passion to help the poor and those struggling through hard times. When the growing season was sluggish, Justin always took the time to explain to me why they were unable to donate. He spoke with his business hat on, but his heartbeat echoed disappointment that he had nothing to offer and that the nearby sheds were empty as well. When Justin did have onions available for donation, he jumped through hoops to expedite the release process to us, sharing our urgency to get food to the people in need as soon as possible.

One time Operation Blessing was hosting a community food-distribution event for which we needed five-pound bags of onions. Justin's onions were stored loose in large cardboard bins, but that did not stop him. He worked diligently behind the scenes to get us a full truckload of onions that were packed in five-pound bags. Justin didn't have to go the extra mile for us, but he did because to him he was providing more than a truckload of onions. He had an urgency to care for people who needed help. Excellent service had always been Justin's trademark, but his delivery of goods that day far surpassed my expectations.

I once visited Justin while in Colorado Springs, Colorado. We talked about business issues over lunch, and then he took extra time to give me a quick tour of the city. In sharing his time with me, Justin let me know that he genuinely valued our relationship. I left that day knowing that I had a partner in the war against poverty, both in mind and in spirit. In today's world of rushed business meetings and hurried client lunches, it is no small thing when a business partner gives you both his time and attention. I did not take that gesture lightly.

Griffin-Holder has since been sold to L&M Companies, and Justin has moved on. Before his departure he took the time to introduce the Operation Blessing staff to our new contacts and to tell them we were his charity of choice. I will always remember Justin and his kindness to me personally and to our organization. I'm so thankful that I had the privilege to be a small part of Justin's world, because he is a giant in mine. His acts of kindness have renewed my hope that there are indeed businesses being run by generous, big-hearted leaders who are committed to working together with nonprofits for the benefit of our communities.

There are also times when we meet people who we know right away have a genuinely sincere heart. You know when someone cares about his or her community by the consistency of the character and integrity demonstrated in his life. Ryan Nece is one such person. This former NFL player's life off the field is a testimony of philanthropic giving that certainly goes well beyond expectations.

Ryan's "You First, Me Second" Generosity

I met Ryan Nece when he was a linebacker for the Tampa Bay Buccaneers. He and I had lunch at a local Tampa restaurant, and he shared with me his passion for helping people, especially kids. We talked about the foundation he had started and his deep desire to make a difference in others' lives through youth scholarships, international service projects, and food giveaways to those in need. We also spent time talking about his mom, his faith, and the impact he wanted to make both on and off the field. It was some time after our first meeting that Ryan and I made another connection. This time he told me about his desire to do something for the kids who had experienced firsthand the devastation of Hurricane Katrina.

Ryan spearheaded a program he named Step Up that brought together his friends and fellow NFL players to supply athletic shoes and clothing to young people who had been affected by the storm. The program allocated players' merchandise from Nike and Reebok to be distributed to storm victims throughout Louisiana, Mississippi, Alabama, and Texas. I was able to assist with the shipment of shoes and clothing to the different distribution points.

Once the merchandise arrived at its destination, I put together a special event so Ryan could be on site to help give the merchandise to Hurricane Katrina victims himself. We chose the location for the distribution: a small community called Baker, just outside Baton Rouge, Louisiana. The event was held inside a big tent, close to one of the larger trailer parks that was housing many of the storm's survivors.

When Ryan arrived at the distribution site, the children greeted him as if he were royalty. Because I knew Ryan personally and realize what a humble man he is, I knew he was embarrassed by the attention. The event was not all about Ryan—it was all about the children and their families who had been through the most incredible uprooting of life imaginable. But Ryan was there, a tangible representation of the generosity that flowed from so many hearts, and it was natural for the children to want to thank him.

I watched Ryan in action as he squatted down to eye level with the little ones and helped them try on different pairs of shoes until they found a perfect fit. I observed Ryan greeting the moms and dads and telling them with sincerity that he was so sorry for their situation. I caught a glimpse every now and then of teenage girls going gaga over him and asking for his autograph.

Ryan took it all in stride because he was not there on his own agenda but rather as a representative of the more than one hundred fifty NFL players who had participated in his Step Up program. Through Ryan's personal efforts in leading the campaign, shoes and clothing were distributed over a four-state region. It was a huge undertaking, but not too large for a man with a heart just as big as the area he reached.

Ryan stayed at the event for a long time to ensure that he would be able to see as many of the children and their families as possible. After the event Ryan still had time in his day to have dinner with a group of us who had been working behind the scenes to make the event happen. One thing I've learned about Ryan is that he is a real person with a heart and mind committed to a "you first, me second" lifestyle. He is definitely a giver, one whose generosity far exceeds the expectations of the people he serves. His life and work are a reminder of how living the right way can make a difference for generations to come.

Living "You First, Me Second"

Do you like surprises? Most of us do. Surprising people is all about giving beyond other people's expectations. It's fun to throw surprise parties for your friends, to celebrate the special occasions of loved ones, to be a part of making memories to be cherished for years to come. But to those who have generous hearts, it can be even more thrilling to surprise people through random acts of kindness. What kinds of random acts? Here are a few ideas for you to consider:

- Have you ever left a cash gift for the housekeeper as you prepared to check out of your hotel?

- Have you ever left a note for the housekeeper saying how much you appreciated the clean room when you checked in?

- When a coworker has been struggling to make ends meet, have you ever left an anonymous cash gift to help him or her out?

- Have you ever offered to trade seats on a flight so a family could sit together?

- If you're a man, do you still open the door for women?

The secret to giving beyond expectations is to look for opportunities. Here are a few suggestions for demonstrating generosity to your coworkers:

- Begin by noticing your coworkers' routines. For instance, by making a mental note of what time the office assistants arrive at work, you can plan to arrive before they do one morning and surprise them with fresh flowers on their desks or by making the first pot of coffee.

- If it's raining outside, find out if anyone has to leave the premises for a scheduled appointment. Ask ahead of time if he or she needs an umbrella.

- If you see someone carrying packages, offer to carry them.

- If someone's car is in the shop, offer transportation assistance.

- Ask the office intern if you can buy him lunch, because you know he has to squeeze six cents out of every nickel.

A few years ago Ryan Nece started a program he calls the Power of Giving. He took seventy envelopes and placed a specific amount of cash in each one. He invited his friends and associates to gather at a restaurant, where he handed each one of them a stuffed envelope with instructions to use the cash to help someone else and to ask the people they helped to perform an act of kindness for someone else in turn. I read an article in Sports Illustrated that said that Ryan's idea had started a charitable chain reaction by which people have become inspired to reach out and help others in spontaneous, creative ways. I'm sure that Ryan would love to hear about random acts of kindness you have participated in. You can share your story at his website www.ryannecefoundation.com. When you are a "you first, me second" giver, I promise that you will never run out of ways to give beyond people's expectations. So whom are you going to surprise first?

Chapter 15

Being Appreciative

Devote yourselves to prayer with
an alert mind and a thankful heart.
Colossians 4:2

SOME OF THE best memories are made when people express appreciation not only verbally but also through their deeds. Many people respond to polite gestures spontaneously by saying thank you, while others prefer to demonstrate their appreciation with a handshake or a hug. Some may express their appreciation through a handwritten note or a formal letter. Still others may express appreciation through awards or public recognition. The ways we share our appreciation are as numerous and as unique as our own personalities. However gratitude is expressed, all of us like to feel appreciated. And we can have the same sense of fulfillment that comes from being appreciated by taking the time to show our appreciation to others.

I am passionate about thanking people. It is in my nature to want to give thanks for even the smallest things. One time I sent a gentleman named Jerry a short note thanking him for spending time with me on the phone. I did not have a working relationship with Jerry, but I was truly thankful that he had taken time out of his schedule to talk with me for so long. About a year later I was visiting Jerry in his office, and he opened his top desk drawer and pulled out the thank-you note that I had written to him one year earlier. He said he kept it because no one else had ever sent him a note thanking him for his time. It took less than five minutes of my time to leave a lasting, positive impression.

Many times those of us in the nonprofit world wait to express appreciation until after we've received the gift we're soliciting. But Jerry reinforced a good lesson for me that day. Appreciation needs to be consistently demonstrated. It acknowledges to people that the gift of their time is just as important as the donation of their tangible goods.

If you work for a nonprofit, you may have sent a letter to a foundation requesting grant funding, and after some time you received a response expressing regret that your request was turned down. Or perhaps you've sent an employment application to a company regarding a job opportunity, and a short time later you received a form letter letting you know that the job is no longer available. Instead of crumpling the letter into a tight paper ball and tossing it across the room in frustration, you may want to consider sending the company a note or a short letter thanking them for their response.

Consider examining the response letter more closely, looking at the reasons the company gave for declining your request, and see if there is any way you can spin a response back to them. I call these rebound letters. Much like when a basketball bounces off the backboard of a basketball hoop and the player retrieves it to make another shot, you too can get the rebounded ball and try the shot again. I sometimes think that this must be where the saying "It's worth another shot" originated. Even if you don't have additional information to offer the company, it might still work to your benefit if you thank them for taking the time to respond to your request and tell them how much you appreciate their consideration. Here is an account about a "rebound letter" that actually turned a negative into a positive.

I once sent a letter of inquiry to the San Francisco 49ers Foundation regarding possible support for our newly developed child obesity health-education program. Unfortunately I received a letter stating that they would consider only projects that specifically targeted children in the Bay Area. After giving the letter some thought, brainstorming some ideas, and making some calls to organizations already working in San Francisco, I was ready to write my rebound letter to offer the foundation some additional options to consider.

I thanked them for the time they had spent reviewing my request, and I suggested additional program options we could offer that would indeed benefit children living in the Bay Area. I explained the details of how we could rework the project to meet the criteria they were looking for. I sent off the rebound letter, and to my great delight, not too long after it was mailed, I received a phone call from the foundation expressing interest in the program changes I had referenced.

In a short period of time a revised nutrition-education program had been put together that would fulfill the requirements the 49ers had for their own community impact goals. I traveled to San Francisco to work out the remaining details and to tailor the program to meet the goals and expectations of the 49ers. It's important to remember when working with any company or established organization that the best programs for community impact are the ones that integrate elements that are important to them.

In our program for the 49ers I was asked if it could include a football theme. I assured them that we could definitely work to make that happen. I spent time brainstorming with some of our team members, and we came up with the idea of taking pictures of food from the various food groups (carbohydrates, protein, fiber, etc.) and putting them inside an image of a football. One of our staff members coined the word *foodball*. The 49ers loved it and spent time creating a nice graphic design that helped the vision of the program become a reality.

My appreciation and respect for the 49ers organization led to a successful relationship merger between us. Our joint efforts to enhance their community service resulted in multiple benefits for children in the San Francisco Bay Area. The appreciation of the 49ers staff was reciprocated toward us as well. To think that such a great relationship merger had evolved from a rebound thank-you letter is a testimony to how important appreciation is in opening doors of opportunity.

There are many ways to show our appreciation when we receive gifts, awards, or accolades, but it is important for us to look at a level of appreciation that extends beyond the value of a gift or an act of kindness demonstrated to you. This is the appreciation and recognition of the incredible worth of the person who is giving the gift. It makes no difference whether the gift comes from a successful company or from an individual living on a fixed income. The value of the person giving the gift is not determined by their monetary worth but in their relationship with you.

You First, Me Second Appreciation

In planning one of my road trips, I knew that it would be important for me to set aside enough time to meet with my contacts at several large corporations in Tennessee. I had a special plaque to present to a pharmaceutical company in recognition of their donations of medicine used in our international medical aid programs, but I intended to include visits with other companies in order to maximize the cost of the airfare, hotel, and rental car. Each of the visits with my corporate contacts was very important, but in my planner I made sure to note that I must stop and visit with Mary Ella.

Mary Ella is a woman in her eighties who has enough love and passion in her heart to warm even the coldest of winter nights. Her hands, robbed of the youth she once knew, display the crippling effects of arthritis. Yet through her pain Mary Ella faithfully hand stitches precious baby blankets for the children who hold a special place in her heart. She knows she may never have a chance to meet these little ones or kiss their tiny foreheads or wrap them up in her homemade blankets, but each little baby remains Mary Ella's motivation to start every day with hope and a purpose.

Each time she has a box of her blankets ready to ship, Mary Ella gives me a call. When she starts to speak, I can always hear an excitement in her voice and sense her great anticipation as she imagines the faces of the babies who will receive a tiny piece of her heart. I am always refreshed following my chats with Mary Ella. There is something soothingly beneficial about spending time with her as she shares her wisdom and insight from life's lessons. People like Mary Ella somehow help give those of us who are on the receiving side of their wisdom a balanced perspective on what is really important and what is not. My time with Mary Ella always results in my being motivated and encouraged to live life to the fullest.

One time shortly after I received a shipment of beautiful baby blankets from Mary Ella, I heard that Kumar, one of our international team members, was on his way to India. I asked him if he had room in his luggage to take a couple of Mary Ella's blankets. Kumar is the kind of person who would purposefully remove items from his suitcase in order to make sure a gift like these blankets would fit. He is a man dedicated to serving others, and his passport and country visas will attest that his dedication for people extends all around the world. Sure enough Kumar was able to deliver Mary Ella's blankets directly into the hands of two young mothers in a small remote village in India, where receiving anything new was a rarity.

Both of the mothers were thrilled to have something so beautiful, and immediately they wrapped their precious little ones in Mary Ella's special creations. Because I had told Kumar about Mary Ella's dedication and her love for children, when he saw the babies wrapped in her blankets, he immediately captured the moment on his camera, taking some incredible pictures. He e-mailed the photos to me from India, and not long after that I was able to place them in special frames and mail them directly to Mary Ella. When she received my package, she called me, crying tears of joy and astonishment that her blankets had been delivered to babies halfway around the world.

If there was one thing I wanted to do for Mary Ella, it was to extend my appreciation for all that she had done for the benefit of others. Her selfless giving motivated me to want to reinforce her value and the importance of her role. She not only blessed the little ones in India with her blankets, but she also extended her love to the babies' mothers, the people of their village, and to everyone else in this special story. The pictures were the perfect way to express my appreciation to Mary Ella with the message that this world is indeed a better place because of her!

There is another type of appreciation that is rich in meaning and significance. It is the kind that is rooted in personal experience. When we successfully live through difficult times or various struggles and then emerge with a new perspective because of lessons we have learned, our appreciation for what we've been through becomes a part of who we are. Then, when we meet someone going through an experience similar to what we have endured, we are able to provide comfort with the statement, "I know how you feel, because it happened to me."

When going through a hardship, there is nothing more soothing than having someone understand your circumstance because they've walked in your shoes. Whenever I meet someone who is going through a financial crisis, I can relate to their struggles, because there was a time when I wondered where I was going to get the money to pay my bills or put food on the table. In time God restored my finances, but the financial devastation became rooted in me so that I could demonstrate empathy and compassion to those who are going through a similar experience.

To quote a paraphrase from 2 Corinthians 1:4, I've heard it said that "God does not comfort us to make us comfortable, but to make us comforters." The comfort I received through my own struggles is the impetus that moves me to extend kindness to others who are going through a similar life experience. My care in such a situation will be particularly meaningful, not only to the person receiving the comfort but also to me personally.

There are so many people who are hurting in our world. Because of our appreciation for being on the other side of a painful experience, the comfort we can offer to others will be laced with hope. Think of those who may have experienced job loss for an extended period or felt the gripping pain of losing a home or endured the loss of a loved one or walked through a painful divorce. The list has no end, because life will always have its share of hard times that always seem to come when we least expect them.

Experiencing life's difficulties can definitely leave battle wounds, but if we can come to appreciate them as "testimony scars," then we'll be ready to be used as a vessel of care for someone else. When people demonstrate care to others because they've been through the same experience, the comfort they are able to give has a deep, intimate meaning.

Recovered and Giving Back

I spent the summer between my junior and senior years in high school living in an unwed mother's home, waiting to birth a baby that I knew was going to be born out of wedlock and put up for adoption. The shame I felt by being put away was almost unbearable to a girl who had just turned seventeen. As I reflect back on that summer, I don't know how I survived, but I made it through.

At the home I was given daily chores. My assigned task was to prepare meal trays three times a day for the girls who had already delivered their babies. These girls were housed in a small hospital section of the home. Each day I placed napkins, silverware, glasses, and plates of food on the trays for breakfast, lunch, and dinner. After I organized the trays, I placed them on a cart, which I wheeled into an elevator and took upstairs into the hospital where the girls who had delivered their babies were staying.

Three times a day I also had to pass by the nursery section, where I could view the newborn babies. I used to look at the tiny little ones through the window, saying to myself that one day it would be my turn. If I could just make it through another day and not give up hope, one day my nightmare would be over.

The months that I stayed at the home were beyond lonely. On many nights my sense of abandonment became suffocating. Not one of my friends from school knew where I was, because I had been forced to make up a tale that I was going to live with my dad in Puerto Rico for the summer. Even though the unwed mothers' home was less than an hour from my house, no one from my family came to visit me except my sister Lynda who, on the day of my departure from the home, brought me a dress to wear when I officially said good-bye to my baby. I felt rejection at the deepest level, and even to this day I can remember the despair I felt as I cried myself to sleep in my own prison of regret.

The experience left deep wounds in me, and it was not until years later, after I was married with children, that I finally found myself ready to give back to others who were suffering the same pain I had endured. One truth I had learned over the years of seeking God's healing over this experience was that it was not going to define me but rather would give my life definition. I wanted my journey through those difficult months to build the kind of character in me that would make a difference in the lives of other girls who were living through the same circumstances. I desired to give these girls the understanding they needed and the hope they deserved.

While living in Texas, I was hired to work as an activities director at an unwed mothers' home. There it was my job to plan and orchestrate indoor activities as well as occasional outings in the local community. I appreciated the opportunity I'd been given to nurture self-worth and esteem into the young women at the home. I thought, "What better person for this job than me?"

I have a deep appreciation for the painful experience I lived through because it has given me the desire to deliver the message that no matter what a person's circumstance, there is always hope for a future. People who have walked in the same shoes as someone who needs help have a great capacity to understand, because they know the person's pain firsthand. They are the ones who can look into the eyes of the hurting and say with great sincerity, "I know how you feel."

Living "You First, Me Second"

Appreciation can be demonstrated on several levels. What makes each level distinct is the amount of time you spend to show your appreciation.

When was the last time someone personally thanked you? A sincere verbal thank you can be just as meaningful as a special card. Why? Because the words are your own and not penned by someone else, and because you are speaking words of encouragement directly to someone else. One secret to being appreciative is slowing down your schedule enough to have the time to actually share your appreciation.

Your goal should be to reinforce the value of the person you are appreciating. In today's world of texting and instant messaging, sending someone a "thnx" does show that you're appreciative, but it does not demonstrate value to a person. In order to do that, more of your time needs to be invested.

Have you ever received a thank-you note that was totally unexpected? Do you remember how you felt after you finished reading it? Some people are so touched by a person taking the time to write them a thank-you card that they keep the card for years. The expression of your gratitude needs to reflect the relationship you have with the person or people you are thanking.

A handwritten thank-you acknowledgment can vary from something penned on a simple piece of paper and put in a plain envelope all the way to a masterfully crafted formal thank-you letter written on your company stationery. It is always important to consider the recipient of your appreciation when choosing the appropriate style of your expression.

If you would like to get better at saying thank you or writing thank-you acknowledgments, try this activity: On your own, designate one week on your personal calendar as appreciation week. Each day of that week make it your goal to express your gratitude to various people in three different ways.

- Say thank you to someone face-to-face, to another one on the phone, and to a third in an e-mail.

- Mark one day on your calendar and designate it for writing someone a short thank-you note. If you are in an office environment and are writing to a coworker, leave the note on her desk or put it in the interoffice mail. If the person is not someone in close proximity to you, then put a stamp on the envelope and drop it in the mail.

- You can also demonstrate appreciation for someone else by doing something that will take more of your time. At the end of your personal appreciation week, take someone out to lunch or dinner, or prepare a special dinner at home for your spouse or family. Put candles on the table and cloth napkins at the place setting. Try to formalize the look of the table just to show that you have invested special thought in your plans.

On your calendar, for every day that you accomplish each act of appreciation, give yourself an A for activating your appreciation! See if you can finish the week with straight As. Take the same idea and repeat your appreciation week the following month. By the time you've had an appreciation week three months in a row, you will be unwilling to wait so long before you start showing appreciation again—or you will more than likely start planning special ways to show appreciation each day. As a matter of fact, you will get to the point where you will not want to keep track of your appreciation moments anymore, because being appreciative will become as natural to you as breathing, and who likes to keep track of that on a calendar?

Finally, for those of you who want to take even greater strides in demonstrating appreciation, spend time thinking about some of your life experiences. Have you experienced times that you thought were so difficult that you might not make it through them? Are there things in your past such as addictions or behaviors that you've conquered or changed? Are you willing to approach others who are currently experiencing those same dark days and offer the kind of hope that only your experience and understanding can bring?

The older I get, the more I realize that every path we tread during our lives, whether by choice or by circumstances beyond our control, can be used to demonstrate care to someone who is experiencing the same thing. When you can come to appreciate the difficult circumstances you've endured in a way that equips you to comfort others, then you will be ready to show "you first, me second" appreciation that will change lives.

Chapter 16

Being a Servant Leader

He sat down, called the twelve disciples over to him, and said, "Whoever wants to be first must take last place and be the servant of everyone else."
Mark 9:35

SERVANT LEADERS ARE people who pound the pavement every day with footsteps dedicated to making a difference in the lives of those they serve. The commitment of servant leaders rises up from hearts that are determined to live out the scripture found in Mark 9:35: they take last place and seek to be the servant of everyone else. The love they freely give knows no boundaries.

Their compassion extends to impact people in their own communities and also reaches out to change the lives of those around the world. Servant leaders work around the clock and remain committed to a job until the work is done. Some servant leaders went to Japan to provide guidance and direction in the restorative process following the massive earthquake and tsunami that occurred there in 2011. More servant leaders went to Haiti determined to provide safe water to those living in tents following the devastating earthquake of 2010.

Others renovated structures following destructive tornadoes that ripped through several US states in April 2011. Some provide aid to people suffering in Africa, while others in Asia seek to create microenterprise programs to empower men and women to provide for their families. You will find servant leaders in Latin America serving orphans and vulnerable children. In every continent around the globe, wherever there are needs, you will find community servant leaders determined to help change people's circumstances and thus better their lives. Wherever there are people who need people, you will find a servant leader.

Servant leaders touch hearts by sending a tangible message that they care. Through their demonstration of tenderness, servant leaders let people know they have value. And when that sense of value is truly embraced, people who may have been teetering on the edge of despair will find new hope. Their discouragement and resignation will turn into optimism and expectation because they realized that someone cares.

By cultivating their own passion for God, servant leaders are in turn able to demonstrate the compassion of God in their acts of love toward their neighbors. They live out principles that I call the BeAltitudes. These values combine the rich character traits described in the Sermon on the Mount (Matt. 5:1–12) with the qualities found in the good Samaritan, a profound example of fulfilling the call to love one's neighbor with unwavering commitment (Luke 10:25–37).

When we demonstrate this combination of character and service to our neighbors in the way God intended, we experience BeAltitude living. These values of loving, serving, and putting the needs of others before your own are found in the hearts of servant leaders. So how are we to live out these BeAltitude values?

Be passionate

God's love for mankind is our model. His unending passion for people is the source of the servant leader's care for others. In Luke 10 when the Samaritan saw the dying man on the side of the road, he stopped to help because he had compassion. This compassion rose up from a well dug deep in his heart by and for God. We are all created with an unending supply of passion for our fellow man. Every time we show "you first, me second" love for our neighbors, that passion is being activated.

Be principle driven

The Samaritan had a choice as to whether he would help the wounded man or mind his own business and continue his journey. The Samaritan's integrity is what led him to minister to needs of the man who had been beaten, robbed, and left for dead. By choosing to stop, he demonstrated his uprightness. In a similar way a servant leader's integrity is clearly seen through his actions.

Be positive

Gentle words of encouragement will bring smiles to people who are struggling to get through devastating circumstances and are on the brink of hopelessness. Surely when the Samaritan knelt down to assure the wounded man that he was there to help, his words must have been like a soothing balm to the man's ears. Just when the man must have thought his life was over, he hears words promising comfort, care, and companionship. When servant leaders display the gentleness of God's compassion, it brings a calming reassurance to those in turmoil, causing them to believe that somehow things are going to be all right.

Be powerful

The "you first, me second" care the Samaritan gave demonstrated power through humility. In putting the needs of another man before his own, the Samaritan illustrated the truth that meekness is at the foundation of loving our neighbor. Meekness is not weakness; it is restrained power. It is *not* doing what you know you could. It is staying when you could leave, remaining silent when you could make a cutting remark. Servant leaders know the power of seeking others' benefit over their own, in remaining silent and allowing their actions to speak on their behalf, and in carefully choosing words that will pump life-saving hope into someone on the brink of despair.

Be persistent

A servant leader must believe that God is always at work, even if circumstances seem to indicate otherwise. The Samaritan walked into the middle of a grave situation, but he did not give up on the injured man. He first cleaned and bandaged the man's wounds, and then he placed the man on his animal to take him to a place of safety. When he found an inn, the Samaritan then cared for the man throughout the night. He could have stopped at any point—when he first met the man, after he'd cleaned his wounds, or once he'd found him a place to stay. But the Samaritan persisted through each step to provide the care the injured man needed. His persistence most assuredly saved a life. Like the Samaritan, a servant leader does not give up easily.

Be partner focused

Because the Samaritan had to go on to Jericho, he needed to call upon another person for help. By getting the innkeeper involved, he created a partnership that was built on trust. The Samaritan was unable to provide the long-term care the injured man needed, but the innkeeper was available and willing. Although the Samaritan did not know how long the man would need to recover, he agreed to return to the inn and cover any expenses incurred during the man's care. When the servant leader is met with responsibilities he cannot handle alone, creating effective partnerships may be the key to getting those needs met in the way that God intends.

Be productive

The Samaritan had been on a journey before he came upon the injured man, and he put his schedule on hold to help this stranger. A productive person is able to accomplish the important things for which he is responsible, even when temporarily sidetracked. Because the Samaritan was willing to take a detour in his plans, the injured man received everything he needed in order to survive. When the Samaritan received the assurance of the man's ongoing care, he continued on his way.

Servant leaders who sacrificially invest themselves to care for suffering people are my heroes. They are today's good Samaritans—men and women who absolutely put the needs of others before their own. One person comes to my mind whose life is a clear demonstration of a "you first, me second" servant leader. This man truly emulates the BeAltitude principles. He is my treasured friend James C. "Jim" Esposito. Jim is the executive director of the New York Christian Resource Center, headquartered in Manhattan.

Truth and integrity define Jim's character. These qualities intertwine to create the core of Jim's being and empower him to fulfill his purpose in life. He is a hands-on leader who commits himself completely to doing whatever it takes to get a job done. He has more friends than anyone can count because the depth of his character and the power of his convictions have made him a people magnet.

Beneath Jim's many good deeds and selfless acts is a man determined to demonstrate the compassion of God. Jim finds opportunities to help others while expecting nothing in return. His acts of kindness have made me want to do more to deliver the message of hope and care to those living in at-risk communities. Jim's work as a servant leader in organizing communities for effective change is dynamic. It is distinctive because of Jim's genuine devotion to the people he serves. He can take a project from start to finish, guaranteeing a brilliant outcome. I have seen Jim in action many times, but one special event stands out in my memory.

Community Impact: Jim's Story

Operation SCORE (Seizing Control of Right Eating) is a community program Jim implemented in a few small pockets of poverty within Harlem, Coney Island, and the lower east side of Manhattan. Operation SCORE, a nutrition-education program Operation Blessing produced, addresses childhood obesity. It is a five-week after-school program that teaches underprivileged children in lower-income neighborhoods about healthy living by showing them how to prepare healthy snacks themselves. Each module in the curriculum focuses on a selected group of foods, and the final unit of study integrates exercise with healthy eating for a winning (SCORE!) lifestyle choice.

When Jim launched the program in New York City, he committed to personally supervising all the Operation SCORE locations to make sure that each child enrolled received the classroom supplies he needed. He conducted the instructor training and personally purchased all the grocery items required for each lesson. During the course of the instruction, teachers and community workers guided the children step-by-step in preparing healthy snacks. At the conclusion of each lesson each child received a bag of groceries containing the exact ingredients needed to prepare several more of the same snacks at home. It was Jim's leadership that ensured the children and instructors had everything they needed for a successful and memorable experience.

The students loved Operation SCORE, so much so, in fact, that their learning followed them home. There they applied leadership skills by teaching their brothers and sisters and even their moms and dads how to prepare fun, healthy snacks! Operation SCORE required a massive amount of oversight, and Jim took ownership of each of the program components as if his life depended on it!

The final lesson of Operation SCORE focused on the importance of exercise. Jim wanted to reinforce to the children the significance of staying healthy through exercise, so he created an unforgettable experience for them. With his creativity and community connections, Jim put together a very special day of fun and fitness that took the children from their inner-city playgrounds to the Hofstra University football field.

There they worked out with players from the New York Jets. Santana Moss, a New York Jets player at the time, helped recruit some of his teammates to participate in the morning's festivities. Jim set up a conditioning circuit with stations manned by Jets players. To dovetail with the Operation SCORE curriculum, each player was given laminated instructions to read to the children as they exercised together.

Jim arranged transportation to the Hofstra field for all the Operation SCORE students and their chaperones. When the children arrived, they were divided into smaller groups and assigned a station where they would begin their circuit. After several minutes of exercise, high-fives, spontaneous hugs, and lots of laughter with the Jets players manning the stations, the children rotated to their next station to start activities with a different player.

Jim placed himself in the center of the field as the official timekeeper. His responsibility was to signal the children's rotation to each new station using a very loud air horn. It was absolutely the most incredible morning that left a lifelong memory in the hearts of every person there.

After completing a full circuit of exercise, the kids posed for pictures with the players and then gathered at the end for a group photo. The children yelled out, "SCORE!", as each picture was taken. After receiving lots of autographs and hugs, the children departed to return to their neighborhoods of uncertainty.

As a special surprise there was another servant leader waiting for the children in the parking lot named Jimmy Mott. He has a full-time job as a cameraman with NBC, but on his days off you will find him giving back to his community and to those he knows have great needs. On this day he delivered a surprise load of grocery bags plus a special turkey for each child to take back to their homes as a blessing for his family.

It clearly takes a village for community service to be most effective, but it also takes Jim Espositos—people dedicated to serving the needs of others, no matter the cost. One of the children from Operation SCORE belted out after the exercise event, "I can't wait till I grow up so I can tell my kids that I worked out with the New York Jets!" Another one yelled, "I'm going to tell my grandkids when I'm an old man! They're never going to believe this!"

Jim Esposito helped to create that memory, because his leadership brought all the puzzle pieces together. I will guarantee that everything Jim does for community impact will carry the same signature of his integrity and brilliance. He is making a difference, one precious life at a time.

Servant leaders willingly invest themselves in people. Their focus is not only on impacting lives but also on finding ways to improve the communities they serve. Because of the combination of their leadership ability and commitment to serve, they are unstoppable when it comes to planning, administrating, executing, and assessing community programs.

Servant leaders are possibly working right now in your own community, perhaps just a short distance from your home. They are tutoring at-risk kids, running food pantries for those who have fallen on hard economic times, and feeding kids hot meals during the summer because schools are closed. Perhaps they fear shutting down because of a lack of support. Perhaps they have been waiting for another community servant leader who will rise up and champion their cause. Will that be you?

Living "You First, Me Second"

Jim had a wonderfully successful event with the New York Jets players at which many of the children he was serving lived out their dreams. If you are considering taking on a leadership role in your community service, here are a few guidelines that Jim followed to ensure the successful outcome of his event:

Clearly define roles

For large-scale community events it is important to provide clear directions for event participants regarding each area of their responsibility. If there are any special instructions, it is imperative that all the event details be covered during a designated training time. The way to guarantee success is to make sure everyone who works at the event is aware of the plan for the day and their responsibilities within that plan.

Provide safety instructions

It is extremely important that safety precautions are taken in order to carry out a successful event, especially when children are involved. If the event environment is unfamiliar or intimidating to the children, a buddy system should be set up so that each child looks after another. If necessary, during training sessions maps should be given to leaders to outline where emergency phones and designated rest areas are located.

- It is important to let all participants know how to dress for the day of the event, particularly which kind of shoes they should wear. If the event will involve a lot of activity, recommend sneakers or shoes with comfortable, flat bottoms.

- It is vital that all event participants have plenty of water to drink, especially when children will be involved in exertive activities. Dehydration can become an issue if the sun is out and the temperature or the humidity is high. You may want to have extra sunscreen available for outdoor events. First-aid kits should also be on hand in case of minor cuts or injuries.

- You may want to consider having an ambulance on site should there be large crowds and high temperatures. Making sure that you plan ahead for any possible emergency is an important part of event planning.

- If the event requires added security measures, the community leader should be proactive in lining up commitments from the police department to provide extra officers for the event, especially if large crowds are anticipated. Police officers will often volunteer their time because of the positive community impact.

Make it a turnkey operation

When businesses want to get involved in social responsibility issues at the community level, they often rely on the experience and expertise of leaders from community-based organizations. If at all possible, a community servant leader should offer to provide a turnkey operation for corporate partners. This means that the community servant commits to carrying the major responsibility for handling the event details, including being on site the day of the event to personally oversee the proceedings.

Successful community servant leaders know what it takes to operate a program that can impact lives and communities to bring positive change. They understand the needs of the people in their own communities, and they know how to meet those needs. By working with a community leader in a turnkey event, a company can meet its goal to make a community connection by serving the people who need it most and by providing a tangible, hands-on, positive experience for all involved.

For those who desire to more effectively reflect servant leader love and compassion as they serve others, consider the following thoughts about the BeAltitude principles to help activate the Good Samaritan in you.

Be passionate

- *Passion involves the heart and embraces the need.* What are the needs among the people or the community you serve?

- *Passion builds a bridge to connect the heart to the need.* Is your heart moved when you see people's needs not being met?

- *God takes passion and gives it purpose.* Have you spent time praying and fasting about the role God wants you to play in meeting people's needs? Are you compelled to make a difference? Do you know why you serve in your community? Are you depending on God for direction?

- *Passion creates momentum and confidence.* Are you motivated? Are you willing to take risks and to make mistakes? Do you know when God's hand is upon you?

Be principle driven

- *The principles you live by will determine how others perceive you.* Is your word your bond?

- *Be consistent in your business or ministry transactions.* Do you consistently serve with integrity even when you don't see immediate results? Do you cut corners or compromise? What do you do when others aren't looking?

- *Remain steadfast when challenged by your opposition.* How do you respond when you are challenged? How would those on your staff describe you?

Be positive

- *Keep a positive attitude in building a team.* Do you value each of your staff members as a vital part of your team? Do you seek the participation of everyone during discussions?

- *Keep the environment positive during challenging times.* Do you focus on the positive or the negative when you face difficulties? Do you rely on others when facing difficulties? Do you find ways to make a difficult situation better?

- *Keep your staff equipped.* Do you provide your staff with the tools they need to accomplish tasks? Is your team's workload shared equitably? Do you reinforce the good things that your staff accomplishes?

Be powerful

- *Humility is power.* Do you insist on primarily having your ideas implemented? Do you put others before yourself? Do you take the credit instead of giving it away?

- *Share your vision with others.* How well can you share with others the vision of what you want to do? Can you articulate your purpose with confidence?

- *Get acquainted with other influential leaders in your community.* Do you spend time getting to know leaders in your community? Do you network? Do you belong to community leadership organizations?

Be persistent

- *Devise a plan, then evaluate it and take action.* Do you recognize that achieving goals and results takes time? Do you assess the approach you are taking to evaluate its effectiveness?

- *Change your strategy to overcome obstacles.* Are you open to changing your approach if it's not working? Is your approach to caring for others open to change? Are your team members unified in supporting your approach?

- *Continually remind yourself of your purpose.* How do you avoid discouragement? Is there unity on your team—are you all one in spirit? Are you committed? How about those around you?

Be partner focused

- *Make a connection that is lasting and mutually beneficial.* Does everyone in your meetings have the same level of input? Do you know your partners' gifts and talents? Do you keep communication open? Do you and your partners work together toward a common goal?

- *Build one another up.* Do you celebrate together with your partners? Are you serving together in one accord? Do you congratulate your partners when they've accomplished a task?

Be productive

Create an IFP (infrastructure for productivity) for being a better servant leader through the following ACTION formula:

- *A* = Approach. Every situation is unique, and you may have to confront adversity. Your reaction to any situation is a choice that only you can make.

- *C* = Confidence. Know what you want to do and how you are going to accomplish your goals. Make sure your plan includes getting others involved if needed.

- **T** = Training. Equip yourself with the tools that will make you successful. Do you have the supplies you need to serve and train effectively?

- **I** = Initiative. Have you made the first move toward your service goals? Are you moving forward? How is your attitude? How is your outlook? Are you a self-starter? Are you using your time wisely so you can get things done?

- **O** = Opportunities. Seize every one that comes. Be alert to your surroundings, strategies, and sources. Be informed of every possibility. Be focused. Be a visionary. Look beyond the limits and see the limitless.

- **N** = Never, ever quit!

Conclusion

And don't forget to do good and to share with those in need. These are the sacrifices that please God.
Hebrews 13:16

A S YOU BEGIN your own "you first, me second" journey, it will be easy for you to become distracted or to be in a hurry and perhaps only think about responding to a need. To help you in your quest to make a difference in this world, there are three important principles to remember: be alert, be available, and take action. Let me give you a brief illustration.

Recently I found myself in a hurry to get to work. When I turned onto the road leading to the parking lot, in my peripheral view I noticed an elderly woman walking slowly while carrying multiple bags. I thought to myself that I was already running late and needed to proceed without delay. I turned in the direction opposite the lady and then watched her in my rearview mirror.

It was only another moment before I realized that I had made a selfish decision and immediately turned the car around and drove back toward the woman, still walking slowly and cautiously with her arms loaded. I pulled up next to her and asked if she needed a ride. She responded, "That would be wonderful."

After she got in the car, I introduced myself, and she told me her name was Grace. She thanked me and then said, "Welcome to God's angel ride brigade." I responded, "Wow, what does that mean?" Grace then shared that she rides the bus every day to work and has to walk quite a ways to get to the building where, as it turns out, we both work. Grace told me that for a long time she had been taking the back way, cutting through grassy areas and remote parking lots. One day she felt God directing her to walk on the front roads and giving her the assurance that He would provide angels to help her.

"So," she said, "God brought you to me today to help me." My eyes filled with tears as I reflected on the incredible blessing I had just received by reaching out to help someone in need.

When you activate the "you first, me second" response, the reward for your service may not only be an encouraged heart; it may be even more than that. Later that day I received an e-mail from Grace in which she shared these words: "It was such a joy to ride with you this morning. Your determination to check if I needed a ride reminds me of the heart of God because He's determined for me to know how much He loves me." Whether we plan ahead of time to help people in need or make spontaneous decisions to demonstrate kindness toward others, we may never know how much our deeds mean to others.

When I first saw Grace, I became alert to her need for help. By putting her needs before my schedule, I made myself available. And finally, by turning the car around, I took the action to respond to her need. Little did I know that I would be the one feeling blessed that morning. Remember to be alert, be available, and take action. When you do, surely God is well pleased.

It has been a joy for me to share with you the stories of people I've had the honor to meet throughout my years of service to others. The people featured in this book are "you first, me second" heroes who are bringing restoration and hope to suffering people in their own communities around the world. Each one of these individuals has inspired me to continue on this journey to serve those who need help the most.

I am passionate about the work I do and the privilege I have to serve as an advocate for people in need. It's my hope that these stories have captured your heart and inspired you to create your own movement to make a difference in your personal sphere of influence.

There are other resources you may find helpful as you apply the "you first, me second" principles discussed in the previous chapters. One of my favorite books is a relationship classic titled *The Tender Commandments* by Dr. Ron Mehl, founder of Compassion Ministries. Dr. Mehl shares insights into building a love relationship between people and their Creator. His book helped me see the incredible opportunities we have to live the commandment "love your neighbor as yourself" out of the fullness we have in our own relationships with God. I wish Dr. Mehl were still alive today so I could tell him personally how his words have impacted my life's work.

Another favorite book of mine is *Living Your Strengths* by Albert Winseman, Donald Clifton, and Curt Liesveld. The book helps readers discover their own God-given strengths and then shows them ways to use their skills and abilities to better serve their communities. I have found this book most useful for discovering people's individual strengths and for creating team-building exercises to help set measures for accountability and team success. This book is a great tool for building confidence within individuals, which enhances their efforts to make connections that help build community.

As you conclude *You First, Me Second*, my desire is that you will be spurred on to love your neighbors in new and innovative ways and that you will demonstrate the love of God through your words and actions. I pray you are inspired daily to live the "you first, me second" life as you deliver hope and value to the people you meet. What an incredible way to change our world!

CREDIBLE, RELEVANT COVERAGE
of the issues that **matter most to you**

FrontLine brings you books, e-books, and other media covering current world affairs and social issues from a Christian perspective. View all of FrontLine's releases at the links below and discover how to bring your values, faith, and biblical principles into today's marketplace of ideas.

FRONT LINE